This book was given to me
Jan 29 - 1931, on my 7 good birthday
by Polly and Jeannette Gath -

The book was written by my old
schoolmate O. T. Corson -

Billy pollok
12ª N 8th
Niles Mich.

PORTRAIT OF LINCOLN

Of all existing paintings of the famous President, many feel that
this profile best reveals the real soul of the great man.

ABRAHAM LINCOLN

His Words and Deeds

By

OSCAR TAYLOR CORSON

LECTURER ON EDUCATION, WESTERN COLLEGE, OXFORD, OHIO
FORMERLY STATE SUPERINTENDENT OF
PUBLIC INSTRUCTION, OHIO
AUTHOR OF "OUR PUBLIC SCHOOLS"

F. A. OWEN PUBLISHING COMPANY
DANSVILLE, N. Y.

CONTENTS

ACKNOWLEDGMENTS

The author's grateful appreciation is hereby expressed to the following publishers for their generous permission to quote, from the volumes named, the selections which are specified in the text and to summarize various incidents and stories:

D. APPLETON AND COMPANY, New York—*Abraham Lincoln*, W. H. Herndon and Jesse W. Weik.

THE BAKER AND TAYLOR COMPANY, New York—*The Life of Abraham Lincoln*, Henry C. Whitney.

THE CENTURY COMPANY, New York—*Abraham Lincoln—A History*, John G. Nicolay and John Hay; *A Short Life of Abraham Lincoln*, John G. Nicolay; *Personal Traits of Abraham Lincoln*, Helen Nicolay; *Lincoln the Lawyer*, Frederick Trevor Hill.

THE CENTURY MAGAZINE, February, 1894—Special permission to quote from article on "Lincoln's Gettysburg Address," by John G. Nicolay.

HOUGHTON MIFFLIN COMPANY, Boston—*Daniel Webster*, Henry Cabot Lodge; *Honest Abe*, Alonzo Rothschild; *The Real Lincoln*, Jesse W. Weik.

J. B. LIPPINCOTT COMPANY, Philadelphia—*The True Abraham Lincoln*, William Eleroy Curtis; *Intimate Character Sketches of Abraham Lincoln*, Henry B. Rankin.

LITTLE BROWN AND COMPANY, Boston—*Tad and His Father*, F. Lauriston Bullard.

THE MACMILLAN COMPANY, New York—*The Life of Abraham Lincoln*, Ida M. Tarbell; *Abraham Lincoln, the Man of the People*, Norman Hapgood.

THE METHODIST BOOK CONCERN (Abingdon Press), New York—*Abraham Lincoln the Christian*, William J. Johnson.

THE PENNSYLVANIA MAGAZINE OF HISTORY AND BIOGRAPHY, October 1909—"The Gettysburg Address," by Major William H. Lambert.

G. P. PUTNAM'S SONS, New York—*Abraham Lincoln, Man of God*, John Wesley Hill.

CHARLES SCRIBNER'S SONS, New York—*History of Andrew Jackson*, Augustus C. Buell.

The Centenary Edition of the Life and Works of Abraham Lincoln, edited by Marion Mills Miller, and published by The Current Literature Publishing Company, is the source of the quotations from Lincoln's letters, addresses, and state papers.

Other volumes which have been carefully read and which are recommended to students of Lincoln are:

Six Months At the White House, F. B. Carpenter.

The Paternity of Abraham Lincoln; The Soul of Abraham Lincoln; and *The Life of Abraham Lincoln*, all by William E. Barton.

Lincoln, Master of Men, Alonzo Rothschild.

Lincoln, Nathaniel Wright Stephenson.

Abraham Lincoln, Lord Charnwood.

Personal Recollections of Abraham Lincoln, Henry B. Rankin.

Abraham Lincoln, George Haven Putnam.

The Boy's Abraham Lincoln, Helen Nicolay.

Gettysburg and Lincoln, Henry Sweetser Burrage.

Lincoln's Gettysburg Address, Orton H. Carmichael.

The Assassination of Abraham Lincoln, and *The Poets' Lincoln*, Osborn H. Oldroyd.

Lincoln in the Telegraph Office, David Homer Bates.

Personal Reminiscences [of Lincoln], L. E. Chittenden.

Uncollected Letters of Abraham Lincoln, Gilbert H. Tracy.

Abraham Lincoln, Defendant, William H. Townsend.

Abraham Lincoln, the Prairie Years, Carl Sandburg.

Lincoln's Parentage and Childhood, Louis A. Warren.

INTRODUCTION

It has been stated that every one who can recall the assassination of President Lincoln has a vivid recollection of all the details connected with the receipt of the news of that terrible tragedy.

The author has interviewed many persons who remember that saddest of all events in our nation's history. Without exception they all testify to the truthfulness of the statement, and are able to tell exactly where they were at the time as well as to give in the minutest detail all the attendant circumstances. This is of itself a most impressive tribute to the memory of the martyred President. It conclusively proves the large place which he occupied in the hearts of the common people of his day.

People who knew Lincoln personally are now few in number. Even those who can remember that fateful fourteenth of April, 1865, when the whole world mourned, form a relatively small portion of the living. And it is feared that the younger generation are not as familiar with his life and character as they should be.

Fortunately, there are many volumes prepared by authors who knew him intimately, which contain a reliable record of his life and work. His letters, speeches, and state papers have been carefully preserved and edited.   In the preparation of this volume all the more important Lincoln literature has been carefully studied.

Credit is also due a number of persons, some of whom are no longer living, who generously accorded the author personal interviews in which they gave freely of their intimate personal knowledge of Lincoln, gained by association with him.   To all such a debt of gratitude is due for their valuable contribution.

Visits to all the important Lincoln shrines have been made in the course of the study, which has covered a period of several years.   In this study there has come an ever deepening impression of the greatness of Lincoln's character together with the conviction that his character can best be revealed and interpreted by what he, himself, said and did.   As Lowell so well describes him:

"Here was a type of the true elder race;
And one of Plutarch's men talked with us face to
    face."

Just as the white light from the sun, when passed through a prism of glass, reveals the seven primary colors of the solar spectrum, so the white light emanating from the soul of Abraham Lincoln, when passed through the prism of a sympathetic study of his words and deeds, reveals the seven primary virtues of his great character—Humility, Reverence, Loyalty, Honesty, Simplicity, Humor, and Magnanimity.   To each of these a chapter is devoted.

In addition a chapter each is given to Lincoln's Education, which was gained by the most persistent effort and intense application; to the Gettysburg Address, which has been and still is so grossly misrepresented as having been delivered with little or no preparation; and to the Lincoln Tomb, about which centers much interesting history not generally known but of sufficient importance to justify its insertion at the close of this book, even if it is not in harmony with the title.

The volume is published with the sincere desire that it may help to create in all who read it a keen appreciation of the rich heritage to be found in the life and character of Abraham Lincoln, of whom his great war secretary, Edwin M. Stanton, declared, at the time of his death,

"Now he belongs to the ages."

Lincoln

Up from log cabin to the Capitol,
One fire was on his spirit, one resolve—
To send the keen ax to the root of wrong,
Clearing a free way for the feet of God,
The eyes of conscience testing every stroke,
To make his deed the measure of a man.
He built the rail-pile as he built the State,
Pouring his splendid strength through every blow;
The grip that swung the ax in Illinois
Was on the pen that set a people free.

From "Lincoln, the Man of the People," in *Collected Works* by Edwin
Markham (in preparation). Used by permission of the author.

ABRAHAM LINCOLN

CHAPTER I

LINCOLN'S HUMILITY

ON February 12, 1809, in the midst of circumstances so disheartening and of conditions so unpromising that it is impossible to realize or even to imagine their effect upon the life of a sensitive child, Abraham Lincoln was born.

> "A blend of mirth and sadness, smiles and tears,
> A quaint knight-errant of the pioneers:
> A homely hero born of star and sod;
> A Peasant Prince; a Masterpiece of God."

By his own unaided efforts, he overcame the effects of the surroundings in which he grew to manhood and won for himself such recognition as made him the great, outstanding, dominating figure of his century. And yet, notwithstanding the great success which he earned and the merited honors which came to him as a result, the keynote of his marvelous life, the secret of his mighty influence was his humility, which enabled him to forget himself in his unselfish desire to serve humanity.

For a third of a century, in the midst of the great slavery contest which stirred the soul of the nation as it had never been stirred before, he was almost constantly before the public eye and in the public thought. And yet, from the time he announced his first candidacy for the Legislature in 1832—a candidacy which resulted in defeat—until that memorable day, the eighth of November, 1864, when he closed his second campaign for the Presidency with a triumphant victory, he never uttered a word or performed a deed which indicated that he ever indulged in any unbecoming exultation because of victory or any unkindly criticism because of defeat.

"I presume you all know who I am. I am humble Abraham Lincoln. I have been solicited by many friends to become a candidate for the Legislature. My politics are short and sweet, like the old woman's dance. I am in favor of a national bank. I am in favor of the internal improvement system, and a high protective tariff. These are my sentiments and political principles. If elected I shall be thankful; if not it will be all the same."

With these simple, direct, and unpretentious statements, this young man of only twenty-three presented his claims to the votes of his constituents with that humility which was to characterize his career throughout life.

About the same time (March, 1832) that this brief announcement of his candidacy was made, in one of the longest letters he ever wrote, he presented somewhat in detail his views on the public questions which interested the people at that time. One of these questions related to the possible need of changes in existing laws. With humility, which might well serve as an example for some legislators of the present day, in both state and nation, who are ever ready to enact new laws or to amend old ones with slight consideration, this young aspirant for legislative honors modestly declared:

"But considering the great probability that the framers of those laws were wiser than myself, I should prefer not meddling with them, unless they were first attacked by others; in which case, I should feel it both a privilege and a duty to take that stand which, in my view, might tend most to the advancement of justice."

The concluding paragraphs of this letter, announcing his first candidacy for public office, reveal in a most interesting manner his ambition to succeed, made worthy by marked humility and modesty combined with rare sincerity and gratitude:

"But, fellow-citizens, I shall conclude. Considering the great degree of modesty which should always attend youth, it is probable I have already been more presuming than becomes me. However, upon the subjects of which I have treated, I have spoken as I have thought. I may be wrong in regard to any or all of them, but, holding it a sound maxim that it is better only sometimes to be right than at all times to be wrong, so soon as I discover my opinions to be erroneous I shall be ready to renounce them.

"Every man is said to have his peculiar ambition. Whether it be true or not, I can say, for one, that I have no other so great as that of being truly esteemed of my fellow-men, by rendering myself worthy of their esteem. How far I shall succeed in gratifying this ambition is yet to be developed. I am young, and unknown to many of you. I was born, and have ever remained, in the most humble walks of life. I have no wealthy or popular relations or friends to recommend me. My case is thrown exclusively upon the independent voters of the county; and, if elected, they will have conferred a favor upon me for which I shall be unremitting in my labors to compensate. But if the good people in their wisdom shall see fit to keep me in the background, I have been too familiar with disappointments to be very much chagrined."

The people, good or bad, or both, did see fit to keep him in the background. He was defeated. But it is most interesting and important to note that Lincoln received six hundred and fifty-seven out of the two thousand one hundred and sixty-eight votes cast in the county, and in his home precinct of New Salem, two hundred and seventy-seven—all but three—of the entire vote. Three months later, in the election for President, the same precinct gave Andrew Jackson one hundred and eighty-five votes, and Henry Clay, whom Lincoln supported, only seventy votes. Considering the fact that he was young and unknown to many of the voters, and that his service in the Black Hawk War made it impossible for him to conduct an extended personal campaign, the vote he received in the county was a fine tribute to his standing and character, while the almost unanimous support he was given at home plainly indicated the confidence reposed in him by his neighbors, who knew him so intimately. It is characteristic of the man that he never ceased to be grateful for this mark of confidence and for the re-

membrance that this was the only time that he was
ever defeated by a direct vote of the people.

This defeat was followed by four successive elections
to the legislature, where he constantly grew in influence each session because of his tactful, forceful,
and intelligent management of both measures and
men. His success in leading to victory the forces
which favored the change of the state capital to Springfield, gave him great prominence in that city which
was to be honored by his future residence. But in all
the success and prominence which came to him, it was
the absence of all self-exaltation and the willingness to
give credit to others in his achievements which secured
for him such a fast hold upon the hearts of the people.

Success in winning these repeated elections to the
legislature was followed by two defeats for the nomination for Congress and one nomination and election to
that body, where he served with his accustomed faithfulness and modesty.

His letters written while in Congress to his intimate
friend and law partner, William H. Herndon, whom
he always addressed as "Dear William," are full of
interest. In these letters can be found no trace of that
feeling of self-importance which sometimes characterizes men who are elected to serve the people but who
forget their duty to their constituents in their admiration of themselves.

"As to speech-making, by way of getting the hang
of the House," he writes, "I made a little speech two
or three days ago on a post office question of no general interest. I find speaking here and elsewhere

about the same thing. I was about as badly scared, and no worse, as I am when I speak in court. I expect to make one within a week or two, in which I hope to succeed well enough to wish you to see it."

Nearly six months later, he refers to what was probably the most important speech he made while in Congress, by saying: "I made an internal-improvement speech day before yesterday, which I shall send home as soon as I can get it written out and printed —and which I suppose nobody will read."

Lincoln was twice defeated for the United States Senate, the first time in 1854 when, as the candidate of the Whig Party, he had forty-five votes to forty-one for the candidate of the Douglas Democrats; and five for Trumbull, an avowed, uncompromising Democrat upon every issue except the Nebraska Bill, in opposition to which he was in agreement with the supporters of Lincoln. Notwithstanding the fact that the supporters of Trumbull were in such a minority, they stubbornly refused to vote for Lincoln who, with generosity and sagacity seldom shown in political strife, urged his supporters to drop his name and to vote for Trumbull. This they did, "though with lingering sorrow," and thereby secured the election of a senator who represented their views upon the question of slavery alone.

It is difficult to realize what this defeat, under such circumstances, meant to Lincoln, to whom an election to the United States Senate must have seemed a most attractive prize. But he never complained or indulged in any unkindly criticism of any one. A few sentences

ABRAHAM LINCOLN

From original negative owned by H. W. Fay, custodian Lincoln Tomb, Springfield, and reproduced by his permission. It is known as the German-Butler-McNulty negative and was taken in Springfield, January, 1861.

LOG CABIN IN WHICH LINCOLN WAS BORN

Three miles from Hodgenville, La Rue County, Kentucky. It was torn down long ago, but the logs were saved. The land has been purchased and a beautiful memorial building erected, inside of which the cabin has been rebuilt.

quoted from a letter to a trusted friend will serve to show his feelings in the matter:

"The agony is over at last, and the result you doubtless know. . . . I regret my defeat moderately, but I am not nervous about it. . . . On the whole, it is perhaps as well for our general cause that Trumbull is elected."

To Lincoln, "the general cause" was always of more importance than his personal success.

On June 16, 1858, Lincoln was declared to be "the first and only choice of the Republicans of Illinois for the United States Senate as the successor of Stephen A. Douglas." In addressing the convention which made this declaration, he delivered a most carefully prepared speech, which opened with the historic statements that were to result in such momentous consequences to both himself and the nation. He said:

"If we could first know where we are and whither we are tending, we could better judge what to do and how to do it. We are now far into the fifth year since a policy was initiated, with the avowed object and confident promise of putting an end to slavery agitation. Under the operation of that policy, that agitation has not only not ceased, but has constantly augmented. In my opinion it will not cease until a crisis shall have been reached and passed. 'A house divided against itself cannot stand.' I believe this government cannot endure permanently, half slave and half free. I do not expect the Union to be dissolved—I do not expect the house to fall—but I do expect it will cease to be divided. It will become all one thing or all the other. Either the opponents of slavery will arrest the further spread of it, and place it where the public mind shall rest in the belief that it is in the course of ultimate extinction; or its advocates will push it forward till it shall become alike lawful in all the States, old as well as new, North as well as South."

On July 24, 1858, Lincoln challenged Douglas to a joint public debate. The challenge was accepted, and the debates followed at Ottawa, Freeport, Jonesboro, Charleston, Galesburg, Quincy, and Alton. That Lincoln entered upon these debates in a spirit of deep earnestness, reverent seriousness, and genuine humility, is shown in a marked manner in the closing sentences of his "Back to the Declaration" speech at Lewistown, Illinois, only four days before the formal opening of the debates:

"Think nothing of me," declared he in one of his impassioned moods,—"take no thought for the political fate of any man whomsoever—but come back to the truths that are in the Declaration of Independence. You may do anything with me you choose, if you will but heed these sacred principles. You may not only defeat me for the Senate, but you may take me and put me to death. While pretending no indifference to earthly honors, I do claim to be actuated in this contest by something higher than an anxiety for office. I charge you to drop every paltry and insignificant thought for any man's success. It is nothing; I am nothing; Judge Douglas is nothing. But do not destroy that immortal emblem of Humanity—the Declaration of American Independence."

Lincoln was again defeated in this contest, because of an antiquated apportionment in the membership of the legislature, which deprived him of his hard-earned victory. The defeat, however, was only temporary.

The contest had revealed his true greatness. Just as success in legislature and Congress had not unduly elated him, so successive defeats for a higher office had not unduly disappointed him. In either success or defeat, he always remained the same "humble Abraham Lincoln," as announced in 1832 in his first candidacy for the legislature.

When asked how he felt over his defeat, he humorously remarked to one friend: "I am like the boy who stubbed his toe. It hurts too bad to laugh and I am too big to cry." But in a letter to another friend, he revealed the humility of his character and, thereby, the foundation of his greatness by saying: "You doubtless have seen ere this the result of the election here. Of course I wished, but I did not much expect, a better result. . . . . I am glad I made the late race. It gave me a hearing on the great and durable question of the age, which I could have had in no other way; and though I now sink out of view, and shall be forgotten, I believe I have made some marks which will tell for the cause of civil liberty long after I am gone."

It was not possible that a man with such a spirit could sink out of view, and he was not forgotten. Instead, in the providence of God, he was soon to become the nation's leader in the hour of its gravest peril and the emancipator of a race. The marks which he had made were indeed to tell for the cause of civil liberty long after he was gone.

On November 6, 1860, he was elected President. Then followed the four months of intense anxiety before he could enter upon his duties as President of the distracted nation, all sections of which he loved with patriotic devotion. These were months of sacred, silent dedication to the great task to which he had been called. The spirit in which he entered upon this task is revealed in the beautiful words spoken, February 11, 1861, to his friends and neighbors as he left his home which he was never to see again:

"MY FRIENDS: No one, not in my situation, can appreciate my feeling of sadness at this parting. To this place, and the kindness of these people, I owe everything. Here I have lived a quarter of a century, and have passed from a young to an old man. Here my children have been born, and one is buried. I now leave, not knowing when or whether ever I may return, with a task before me greater than that which rested upon Washington. Without the assistance of that Divine Being who ever attended him, I cannot succeed. With that assistance, I cannot fail. Trusting in Him who can go with me, and remain with you, and be everywhere for good, let us confidently hope that all will yet be well. To His care commending you, as I hope in your prayers you will commend me, I bid you an affectionate farewell."

This same spirit of humility, claiming little for himself, trusting in God for guidance and assistance, and relying upon the people for sympathy and support, manifested itself in his every utterance on his journey to Washington.

At Columbus, Ohio, on February 13, he said:

"I cannot but know what you all know, that without a name, perhaps without a reason why I should have a name, there has fallen upon me a task such as did not

rest even upon the Father of his Country; and so
feeling, I can turn and look for that support without
which it will be impossible for me to perform that
great task.   I turn, then, and look to the American
people, and to that God who has never forsaken them."

At Steubenville, Ohio, the following day:

"I fear that the great confidence placed in my ability is unfounded.   Indeed, I am sure it is. . . .
If I adopt a wrong policy, the opportunity for con-
demnation will occur in four years' time.   Then I can
be turned out, and a better man with better views put
in my place."

At Pittsburgh, February 15:

"By the Constitution, the executive may recommend
measures which he may think proper, and he may veto
those he thinks improper, and it is supposed that he
may add to these certain indirect influences to affect
the action of Congress.   My political education strongly inclines me against a very free use of any of these
means by the executive to control the legislation of
the country.   As a rule, I think it better that Congress
should originate as well as perfect its measures without external bias."

On the same day at Cleveland, he addressed a great
crowd of people who had marched or stood in the rain
for two hours awaiting his train:

"The large numbers that have turned out under
these circumstances testify that you are in earnest
about something, and what is that something?   I
would not have you suppose that I think this extreme
earnestness is about me.   I should be exceedingly
sorry to see such devotion if that were the case.   But
I know it is paid to something worth more than any

one man, or any thousand or ten thousand men. You have assembled to testify your devotion to the Constitution, to the Union, and the laws, to the perpetual liberty of the people of this country."

Before the New York Legislature at Albany, February 18:

"It is true that while I hold myself, without mock modesty, the humblest of all individuals that have ever been elevated to the Presidency, I have a more difficult task to perform than any one of them."

In Independence Hall, Philadelphia, early in the morning of Washington's birthday, he took part in raising a new flag, and said:

"All the political sentiments I entertain have been drawn, so far as I have been able to draw them, from the sentiments which originated in and were given to the world from this hall. I have never had a feeling, politically, that did not spring from the sentiments embodied in the Declaration of Independence. . . I have often inquired of myself what great principle or idea it was that kept this Confederacy so long together. It was not the mere matter of separation of the colonies from the motherland, but that sentiment in the Declaration of Independence which gave liberty not alone to the people of this country, but hope to all the world, for all future time. . . . This is the sentiment embodied in the Declaration of Independence. Now, my friends, can this country be saved on that basis? If it can, I will consider myself one of the happiest men in the world if I can help to save it. . . . But if this country cannot be saved without giving up that principle, I was about to say I would rather be assassinated on this spot than surrender it."

On the afternoon of the same day, at Harrisburg, Lincoln related his experiences of the morning in Independence Hall and then added:

"Our friends there had provided a magnificent flag of the country. They had arranged it so that I was given the honor of raising it to the head of its staff, and when it went up I was pleased that it went to its place by the strength of my own feeble arm. When, according to the arrangement, the cord was pulled, and it floated gloriously to the wind, without an accident, in the bright, glowing sunshine of the morning, I could not help hoping that there was in the entire success of that beautiful ceremony at least something of an omen of what is to come. Nor could I help feeling then, as I have often felt, that in the whole of that proceeding I was a very humble instrument. I had not provided the flag; I had not made the arrangements for elevating it to its place; I had applied but a very small portion of even my feeble strength in raising it. In the whole transaction I was in the hands of the people who had arranged it, and if I can have the same generous co-operation of the people of this nation, I think the flag of our country may yet be kept flaunting gloriously."

It is impossible to imagine the emotions which must have stirred the humble soul of Abraham Lincoln as he closed his First Inaugural Address with the immortal words so expressive of his sympathetic, generous, forgiving spirit:

"In your hands, my dissatisfied fellow-countrymen, and not in mine, is the momentous issue of civil war. The government will not assail you. You can have no conflict without being yourselves the aggressors. You have no oath registered in heaven to destroy the government, while I shall have the most solemn one 'to preserve, protect, and defend it.'

"I am loath to close. We are not enemies, but friends. We must not be enemies. Though passion may have strained, it must not break our bonds of affection. The mystic chords of memory, stretching from every battlefield and patriot grave to every living heart and hearthstone all over this broad land, will yet swell the chorus of the Union when again touched, as surely they will be, by the better angels of our nature."

The Gettysburg Address has well been described as being unique not only for what it contains but also for what it omits. It gives, in the small compass of only two hundred and sixty-eight words, one hundred and ninety-six of which are words of one syllable, the most complete and eloquent expression ever recorded of the ideals of free government and of the purposes of a civil war waged in its defense, together with the most touching tribute ever spoken in memory of the soldier dead. It omits everything of a harsh, unkind, or critical nature, as well as everything suggestive of personal exaltation or triumph. No pronoun of the first person, singular number, mars the unsurpassed beauty of the unrivaled diction of this prose poem, which breathes the spirit of humility in every line. In this immortal address, Lincoln reached the heights of sublimity through the depths of humility, when he said:

"But, in a larger sense, we cannot dedicate—we cannot consecrate—we cannot hallow this ground. The brave men, living and dead, who struggled here, have consecrated it far above our poor power to add or detract. The world will little note, nor long remember what we say here, but it can never forget what they did here."

In the early hours of the morning of November 9, 1864, Lincoln left the War Department, where he had gone the evening before to receive the news of his triumphant re-election to the Presidency. A feeling of exultation on his part would certainly have been pardonable, under the circumstances. But no such feeling possessed him. On the contrary, his mind and heart were overflowing with humility, gratitude, and generosity, as indicated by his remarks to a group of serenaders who greeted him:

"I am thankful to God for this approval of the people; but, while deeply grateful for this mark of their confidence in me, if I know my heart, my gratitude is free from any taint of personal triumph. I do not impugn the motives of any one opposed to me. It is no pleasure to me to triumph over any one."

A few days after these words were spoken, the great President found time in his busy life to write the historic letter to Mrs. Bixby, a framed copy of which adorns the walls of one of the colleges of Oxford University, England—placed there by the direction of the faculty of that great institution, as being the finest specimen of English ever written. But it is much more than a fine specimen of English. It reveals in a marked manner the heart of humility which characterized Lincoln, who would not presume to intrude his own personality upon the grief-stricken mother, but with rare delicacy tendered to her the consolation that could be found in the thanks of the Republic her five sons had died to save.

Lincoln's Letter to Mrs. Bixby

"I have been shown in the files of the War Department a statement of the Adjutant-General of Massachusetts that you are the mother of five sons who have died gloriously on the field of battle. I feel how weak and fruitless must be any words of mine which should attempt to beguile you from the grief of a loss so overwhelming. But I cannot refrain from tendering to you the consolation that may be found in the thanks of the Republic they died to save. I pray that our Heavenly Father may assuage the anguish of your bereavement, and leave you only the cherished memory of the loved and lost, and the solemn pride that must be yours to have laid so costly a sacrifice upon the altar of freedom."

On March 1, 1865, the usual congressional committee waited upon President Lincoln and formally notified him of his re-election by the electoral college. To this notification he responded by reading the following brief address expressive of the same humility, gratitude, and generosity manifested in his informal remarks to the friends who greeted him on the morning of November 9:

"With deep gratitude to my countrymen for this mark of their confidence; with a distrust of my own ability to perform the duty required under the most favorable circumstances, and now rendered doubly difficult by existing national perils; yet with a firm reliance on the strength of our free government, and the eventual loyalty of the people to the just principles upon which it is founded; and above all, with an unshaken faith in the Supreme Ruler of Nations, I accept this trust."

No more sublime utterances ever fell from the lips of a human being than those contained in the Second Inaugural Address of President Lincoln, delivered on March 4, 1865, "in a diction rivaling the fire and dignity of the old Hebrew prophecies," to quote a phrase from Nicolay and Hay. In this Inaugural, one of the briefest in our history, the President contrasts the conditions existing at the time of his first inauguration and the present one; discusses in a few comprehensive sentences the relation of the war to slavery; calls attention to the unexpected duration of the war to both the North and the South; and then, in the most humble and forgiving spirit, declares his belief in "the eternal law of compensation," and closes with these words of appeal:

"With malice toward none, with charity for all, with firmness in the right, as God gives us to see the right, let us strive on to finish the work we are in; to bind up the nation's wounds; to care for him who shall have borne the battle, and for his widow, and his orphan—to do all which may achieve and cherish a just and lasting peace among ourselves, and with all nations."

It was in reply to the congratulations of his friend, Thurlow Weed, upon his notification speech and inaugural address, that Lincoln expressed his own views of that address with characteristic frankness, simplicity, and humility:

"Every one likes a compliment. Thank you for yours on my little notification speech and on the recent inaugural address. I expect the latter to wear as well as—perhaps better than—anything I have produced; but I believe it is not immediately popular. Men are not flattered by being shown that there has been a difference of purpose between the Almighty and them. To deny it, however, in this case, is to deny that there is a God governing the world. It is a truth which I thought needed to be told, and, as whatever of humiliation there is in it falls most directly on myself, I thought others might afford for me to tell it."

On April 9, 1865, came the surrender at Appomattox, which was a prophecy of the near approach of the end of the war whose burdens Lincoln had borne for four years with unspeakable sadness and anxiety. The few days still allotted to him to live were days of happy relief from the long strain to which he had been subjected. The fateful fourteenth of April was one of the happiest days of his entire life. His mind was busy with plans for the full restoration of the Union, which he hoped soon to see realized, and his heart was overflowing with gratitude "free from any taint of personal triumph." But that happy day was to be followed by the saddest night in our nation's history— the night which witnessed the assassination of Abraham Lincoln, the kindest man the world has ever known.

For the first time the telegraph was used to carry to the world the tidings of a tragedy which produced world-wide sorrow, in the midst of which the victory

at Appomattox was, in a large measure, lost sight of.
As a result, there was no organized expression of rejoicing over the downfall of the rebellion. And as
we think of Lincoln's humility, hearty accord will be
given to the statement of John G. Nicolay, his private
secretary and biographer in his *A Short Life of Abraham Lincoln:*

"It was unquestionably best that it should be so; and
Lincoln himself would not have had it otherwise. He
hated the arrogance of triumph; and even in his cruel
death he would have been glad to know that his passage to eternity would prevent too loud an exultation
over the vanquished."

It was the belief of John Ruskin that the first test
of a truly great man is his humility. In all the experiences of his life, Abraham Lincoln met and perfectly
passed this test. As a result, he is to-day enshrined in
the hearts of millions of the so-called common people,
who love him and who revere his memory because
they know that his great heart always beat true in the
common cause of a common humanity.

On each recurring anniversary of his birth, in ever-
increasing numbers, children in the public schools
study with interest and profit the story of his early
struggles with poverty and misfortune; students in
colleges are encouraged to persevere in their work by
his experience in educating himself practically without
the help of either schools or teachers; people of all
classes and conditions, in homes and churches and
great mass meetings and banquet halls, unite in paying tribute to his memory and in pledging anew their

allegiance to the principles for which he lived and died.

We honor ourselves in gratefully acknowledging the debt of gratitude we owe him. And we can immeasurably bless our own lives, as well as all the lives we touch by our influence, by dedicating ourselves body, mind, and soul to the high ideals of service proclaimed more than nineteen hundred years ago by the Lowly Nazarene and so perfectly exemplified in the life of humility lived by Abraham Lincoln.

"Whosoever will be great among you let him be your minister.

"And whosoever will be chief among you let him be your servant."

CHAPTER II

LINCOLN'S REVERENCE

THE preceding chapter furnishes conclusive evidence of Lincoln's Humility—that dominant quality of his great soul which was the controlling factor in all that he said and did.

Closely related to Humility, that lowliness of mind which leads all who possess it in a reasonable degree to esteem others better than themselves, is Reverence, another soul quality which recognizes that there are some things in the world which are sacred and, therefore, worthy of veneration and worship. Reverence cannot exist without humility. Humility naturally begets reverence. As has been truly said:

"Reverence is one of the signs of strength; irreverence one of the surest indications of weakness. No man will rise high who jeers at sacred things. The fine loyalties of life must be reverenced or they will be forsworn in the day of trial."

The pages of history record many incidents which illustrate the ennobling effects of reverence, and also, sad to relate, the destructive influence of irreverence upon human life and character.

In 1836 Aaron Burr died in poverty and obscurity. His life began with the most brilliant promise. It ended in the most dismal failure. When Andrew Jackson, beneath whose rough exterior there was a truly reverent soul, learned of Burr's death, he remarked to Francis P. Blair, one of his most intimate friends, who was afterwards a cordial supporter of President Lincoln:—

"Burr came within one trait of exalted greatness." Upon being asked by Mr. Blair what trait that was, he replied:

"Reverence, sir, reverence. I don't care how smart or how highly educated, or how widely experienced a man may be in this world's affairs, unless he reveres something and believes in somebody beyond his own self, he will fall short somewhere. That was the trouble with Burr. I saw it when I first met him at Philadelphia in 1796. . . . . . . I liked him and for many things admired him. But I never could get over that one impression that he was irreverent. And that was what stood in his way. . . . . . Yes, Blair, a man must revere something, or no matter how smart or brave he is, he will die as Burr died in New York the other day, friendless and alone."

Reverence, which was sadly lacking in Aaron Burr, to whom nothing seemed sacred either in life or government, Abraham Lincoln possessed in an unusual degree and constantly manifested in all his life both private and public.

After he was nominated for the Presidency in 1860 and was asked to furnish material for a history of his life, he replied that his early life could all be con-

HOME OF LINCOLN, SPRINGFIELD, ILLINOIS

SCENE AT THE TIME OF THE LINCOLN-DOUGLAS DEBATES

One of the debates between Lincoln and Douglas was held in 1858
at Galesburg, Illinois, the seat of Knox College.

densed into one sentence, found in Gray's Elegy—
"The short and simple annals of the poor." While
this is literally true, he revered the memory of his
mother, who died when he was only nine years old,
and he was always reverently considerate of his step-
mother, who was a woman of unusually strong character and deeply devoted to his welfare. His love for
her was shown in many ways but in none more striking than in his last visit with her before he left to assume his duties as President. With the tears stream-
ing down her cheeks, she gave him her parting bene-
diction mingled with an expression of fear that his life
might be taken by his enemies and that she might
never see him again. After her fears had been realized, she paid him the loving tribute of her heart
by saying:

"He was the best boy I ever saw or expect to see."

Lincoln also revered the cardinal virtues, which
are the foundation of all true character, such as truth,
honesty, and sincerity. It is related of him that one
morning when he was on his way to the woods with
his ax on his shoulder, he was followed by his young
stepsister, 'Tilda Johnston, who had been forbidden
by her mother from accompanying him. With true
girlish enthusiasm she silently slipped up behind her
big brother, who was singing on his way to his work,
and with a cat-like leap jumped squarely on his back
and succeeded in throwing him to the ground. In the
fall, the sharp ax inflicted an ugly wound on 'Tilda's
ankle from which the blood flowed freely. When the

wound was rudely bound up by a generous use of the brother's scanty wardrobe, and the sister's fright had somewhat subsided, he said:*

" 'Tilda, what are you going to tell Mother about getting hurt?"

"Tell her I did it with the ax," sobbed the sister. "That will be the truth, won't it?" To which her brother replied:

"Yes, that's the truth, but it is not all the truth. Tell the whole truth, 'Tilda, and trust your good mother for the rest."

"Telling the whole truth" and "trusting for the rest" to the justice which truth ultimately brings, was characteristic of Lincoln's entire life. Because of this characteristic, he would not—he could not, in his law practice, defend any one who willfully misrepresented the facts. To one client who unfolded to him the details of a dubious claim, which he pressed in a proposed suit he said:†

"Well, you have a pretty good case in technical law, but have a pretty bad case in equity and justice. You'll have to get some one else to win it for you. I couldn't do it. All the time while standing before the jury, I'd be thinking, 'Lincoln, you're a liar'; and I believe I should forget myself and say it out loud."

On another occasion, the same author tells us, he became so disgusted with the evidently false statements made by a client on the witness stand that he arose and left the court room. The judge in charge of the

*Abraham Lincoln, by Herndon and Weih.
†Honest Abe, by Rothschild.

case sent the sheriff to the hotel, where Lincoln had gone, to call him back. When Lincoln was informed that the judge wanted him to return, he replied: "Oh, does he? Well, you go back and tell the judge that I can't come. My hands are dirty and I came over to clean them."

He would not return, and the untruthful client lost his case.

It was reverence for the truth that led Lincoln, on July 17, 1858, to make his celebrated "house-divided-against-itself" speech, in opposition to the advice and protest of many of his closest friends. To their suggestion that it would defeat him in his contest with Douglas for the United States Senate, he replied:

"This thing has been retarded long enough. The time has come when these sentiments should be uttered, and if it is decreed that I should go down because of this speech, then let me go down linked with the truth —let me die in the advocacy of what is just and right."

Lincoln's profound reverence for the truth and his intense loyalty to the truth influenced in a great degree both his thinking and his expression of thought. This is clearly revealed in a beautiful tribute to his memory by President J. M. Sturtevant of Illinois College, who says:

"I knew Mr. Lincoln very well, I may say somewhat intimately, before he was ever thought of in connection with the exalted station to which he was afterwards elected. In those years of his comparative obscurity, I knew him as pre-eminently a truthful man. His love of truth was conspicuous in all his thinking.

The object of his pursuit was truth, and not victory in argument or the triumph of his party, or the success of his own cause. This was always conspicuous in his conversation. It constituted the charm of his conversation. In his society one plainly saw that his aim was so to use words as to express and not to conceal his real thoughts. This characteristic had formed his style, both of conversation and of writing. His habitual love of truth had led him successfully to cultivate such a use of language as would most clearly and accurately express his thoughts. His words were a perfectly transparent medium through which his thought always shone out with unclouded distinctness. No matter on what subject he was speaking, any person could understand him. This characteristic of his mind and heart gave a peculiar complexion to his speeches, whether at the bar, or in discussing the great political issues of the time."

Lincoln's reverence for the Constitution is in striking contrast to the lack of respect shown for it by those to whom age either of a person or a government seems to be an object of derision and contempt. To opinionated egotism and bigoted self-conceit ever ready to speak and act out of the abundance of ignorance or the "arrogance of inexperience," the Constitution may appear to be only an ordinary document, unworthy of respect even if it has stood the severe test of time and proved its perfect adaptability to the growing needs of an advancing civilization—a document to be amended without serious consideration, upon the slightest pretext or to be ignored or nullified at the demands of lawlessness and selfishness. To Lincoln's well-trained mind, ripened judgment, and reverent soul, the Constitution was the sacred charter of our government, worthy of the highest respect and veneration.

On June 20, 1848, in a speech made in the Congress of the United States, on the subject of Internal Improvements, Lincoln said:

"I wish now to submit a few remarks on the general proposition of amending the Constitution. As a general rule, I think we would much better let it alone. No slight occasion should tempt us to touch it. Better not take the first step which may lead to a habit of altering it. Better, rather, habituate ourselves to thinking of it as unalterable. It can scarcely be made better than it is. New provisions would introduce new difficulties, and thus create and increase appetite for further change. No, sir: let it stand as it is. New hands have never touched it. The men who made it have done their work, and have passed away. Who shall improve on what *they* did?"

With such reverence for the Constitution, the fundamental law of the land, it is not surprising that he always manifested the deepest reverence for laws enacted in accordance with its provisions. To Lincoln all laws, divine or human, were sacred.

His reverence for law was publicly declared more than a decade before he made his famous "remarks on the general proposition of amending the Constitution." On January 27, 1837, when only twenty-eight years of age, he delivered his remarkable address on "The Perpetuation of Our Political Institutions" be-

fore the Young Men's Lyceum of Springfield, Illinois
—a society organized by Lincoln and other young men
in the fall of 1836. This address has been the subject
of adverse criticism by at least one of Lincoln's recent
biographers, who refers to it as a "mere rhetorical
stunt, in his worst vein, and deservedly forgotten."
The answer to all such criticism is found in the fact
that, notwithstanding the address was made in 1837—
ninety years ago—it is still constantly referred
to and quoted from as having a direct bearing upon
present-day conditions. Long after the author of
such criticism is dead and forgotten, the address will
live and be remembered because it strongly empha-
sizes the importance and necessity of reverence for
law and obedience to law, both of which are absolutely
essential to the life of any government.

In the opening paragraph of this address, attention
is called to the indisputable fact that the people of this
nation are the legal inheritors of the fundamental
blessings of civil and religious liberty bequeathed as
a legacy by the fathers who had purchased them at the
cost of self-sacrifice and sometimes of even life itself. It was, therefore, the task of each generation
to transmit these blessings to the next, and so on to
"the latest generation that fate shall permit the world
to know." "This task," declared Lincoln, "gratitude
to our fathers, justice to ourselves, duty to posterity,
and love for our species in general, all imperatively require us faithfully to perform."

It was Lincoln's belief that whatever grave dangers
threatened to interfere with the performance of this

task, were within, rather than without the Republic, and he declared:

"If destruction be our lot we must ourselves be its author and finisher. As a nation of freemen we must live through all time or die by suicide."

Even then he called attention to "something of ill omen amongst us—the increasing disregard for law which pervades the country—the growing disposition to substitute the wild and furious passions in lieu of the sober judgment of courts, and the worse than savage mobs for the executive ministers of justice." The remedy he proposed then is the remedy needed now—the only remedy which will ever cure lawlessness:

"Let every American, every lover of liberty, every well-wisher to his posterity swear by the blood of the Revolution never to violate in the least particular the laws of the country, and never to tolerate their violation by others. As the patriots of seventy-six did to the support of the Declaration of Independence, so to the support of the Constitution and laws let every American pledge his life, his property, and his sacred honor—let every man remember that to violate the law is to trample on the blood of his father, and to tear the charter of his own and his children's liberty. Let reverence for the laws be breathed by every American mother to the lisping babe that prattles on her lap; let it be taught in schools, in seminaries, and in colleges; let it be written in primers, spelling-books, and in almanacs; let it be preached from the pulpit, proclaimed in legislative halls, and enforced in courts of justice. And, in short, let it become the political religion of the nation; and let the old and the young, the rich and the poor, the grave and the gay of all sexes and tongues and colors and conditions, sacrifice unceasingly upon its altars."

The primary cause of lawlessness in any nation is a lack of reverence for law, which can be corrected only by the united and persistent effort of homes, schools, churches, newspapers, law makers, and courts in insisting that all constitutionally enacted laws are sacred, should be reverenced, and must be enforced.

Reverence for the Constitution and the laws of the Republic naturally leads to reverence for the rights which the Constitution and the laws were adopted and enacted to protect. These rights include human rights and property rights—the rights of both labor and capital, all of which stand or fall together.

It is not uncommon to hear or to read statements of a radical nature, relative to these rights, which are credited to Lincoln—statements which he never made and which any student of his life and character would at once recognize as being a part of false propaganda on the part of some one who was attempting to secure support for a wrong cause by misrepresenting Lincoln's attitude toward that cause. He is often quoted as having prophesied "the ruinous reign of the money power," and in various ways attempting to incite a warfare between capital and labor. Nothing could be farther from the truth. His attitude toward both labor and property is definitely stated in his "Remarks on the Interest of Labor in Respecting Rights of Property," made March 21, 1864, to a Committee from the Workingmen's Association of New York:

"The strongest bond of human sympathy, outside of the family relation, should be one uniting all working people, of all nations, and tongues, and kindreds. Nor should this lead to a war upon property, or the owners of property. Property is the fruit of labor; property is desirable; is a positive good in the world. That some should be rich shows that others may become rich, and hence is just encouragement to industry and enterprise. Let not him who is houseless pull down the house of another, but let him work diligently and build one for himself, thus by example assuring that his own shall be safe from violence when built."

Whenever Abraham Lincoln is quoted as being on the wrong side of any great moral issue or as expressing radical views regarding any great social or economic question, it is always safe to conclude that he has been misquoted either because of ignorance, which is inexcusable, or because of a purpose to deceive, which is criminal.

Charges have been made from time to time that Lincoln was an agnostic, an infidel, and an atheist. Usually such charges have originated with men who were, themselves, skeptically inclined, and who evidently desired to place Lincoln in their class because of the support which his name would bring to their cause. The refutation of all such charges is found in Lincoln's life as revealed in his words and deeds, which prove beyond doubt that he was a man of profound faith in God and of the deepest reverence for everything associated with His name.

His reverence for the Bible is shown not only in

the manner and the frequency with which he quoted from its pages but also in what he said about it on different occasions.

On September 7, 1864, in accepting a Bible presented by a committee of colored people from Baltimore, he said:

"In regard to this great book, I have but to say it is the best gift God has given to man.

"All the good Savior gave to the world was communicated through this book. But for it we could not know right from wrong. All things most desirable for man's welfare, here and hereafter, are to be found portrayed in it."

In the summer of 1864, Lincoln and his family lived for a short time at the Soldiers' Home near Washington. While there his life-long friend, Joshua Speed, visited them. Upon entering the room he found the President sitting near a window reading his Bible, and remarked that he was glad to see him "so profitably engaged." To this Lincoln replied, "Yes, I am profitably engaged," and then in one terse statement, which revealed his belief in and reverence for the Bible, he suggested how it should be read:

"Take all of this book upon reason that you can, and the balance on faith, and you will live and die a happier man."

Lincoln's addresses, messages to Congress, and other state papers, are filled with statements which plainly indicate his reverence for the Bible and for the God therein revealed. In his First Inaugural Address, he declared:

"Intelligence, patriotism, Christianity, and a firm reliance on Him who has never yet forsaken this favored land, are still competent to adjust in the best way all our present difficulty."

Four years later, in his Second Inaugural Address, with his reverent soul chastened by four years of terrible agony due to civil war between the North and South, both of which he passionately loved, his reverence again manifests itself as he declares:

"The Almighty has His own purposes. 'Woe unto the world because of offences! for it must needs be that offences come; but woe to that man by whom the offence cometh.' If we shall suppose that American slavery is one of those offences which, in the providence of God, must needs come, but which, having continued through His appointed time, He now wills to remove, and that He gives to both North and South this terrible war, as the woe due to those by whom the offence came, shall we discern therein any departure from those divine attributes which the believers in a living God always ascribe to Him? Fondly do we hope — fervently do we pray — that this mighty scourge of war may speedily pass away. Yet, if God wills that it continue until all the wealth piled by the bondman's two hundred and fifty years of unrequited toil shall be sunk, and until every drop of blood drawn with the lash shall be paid by another drawn with the sword, as was said three thousand years ago, so still it must be said, 'The judgments of the Lord are true, and righteous altogether.' "

In response to a resolution by the Senate of the United States that the President be requested "to designate and set apart a day for national prayer and humiliation," Lincoln issued his Proclamation of March 30, 1863, in which he gave indisputable evidence of his deep reverence and profound faith. In this Proclamation attention is called to "the duty of nations as well as of men to own their dependence upon the overruling power of God; to confess their sins and transgressions in humble sorrow, yet with assured hope that genuine repentance will lead to mercy and pardon; and to recognize the sublime truth, announced in the Holy Scriptures and proved by all history, that those nations only are blessed whose God is the Lord."

Declaring his belief that "nations, like individuals, are subjected to punishments and chastisements," he inquires whether "we may not justly fear that the awful calamity of civil war which now desolates the land may be but a punishment inflicted upon us for our presumptuous sins, to the needful end of our national reformation as a whole people."

He then recites how the people of the United States had been "the recipients of the choicest bounties of Heaven"; how they "had been preserved, these many years, in peace and prosperity"; how they had "grown in numbers, wealth, and power as no other nation has ever grown." And then, with a keen realization of the effects produced by material success, he adds:

"But we have forgotten God. We have forgotten the gracious Hand which preserved us in peace, and multiplied and enriched and strengthened us; and we have vainly imagined, in the deceitfulness of our hearts, that all these blessings were produced by some superior wisdom and virtue of our own. Intoxicated

with unbroken success, we have become too self-suffi-
cient to feel the necessity of redeeming and preserving grace, too proud to pray to the God that made us.

"It behooves us, then, to humble ourselves before
the offended power, to confess our national sins, and
to pray for clemency and forgiveness."

The closing paragraph of this remarkable Proclamation named April 30, 1863, "as a day of national humiliation, fasting, and prayer" and requested "all the
people to abstain on that day from their ordinary sec-
ular pursuits, and to unite at their several places of
public worship and their respective homes in keeping the day holy to the Lord, and devoted to the humble discharge of the religious duties proper to that
solemn occasion."

Lincoln reverenced the Sabbath Day.   He was a
regular attendant upon the services of the church both
in Springfield and Washington.   His order for Sabbath Observance issued November 15, 1862, plainly
indicates both his reverence for the day and his belief
in the importance of its sacred observance.   In that
order he says:

"The President, Commander-in-chief of the Army
and Navy, desires and enjoins the orderly observance
of the Sabbath by the officers and men in the military
and naval service.   The importance for man and beast
of the prescribed weekly rest, the sacred rights of
Christian soldiers and sailors, a becoming deference
to the best sentiments of a Christian people, and a
due regard for the Divine will, demand that Sunday
labor in the army and navy be reduced to the measure
of strict necessity.   The discipline and character of

the national forces should not suffer, nor the cause they defend be imperilled, by the profanation of the day or name of the Most High."

Lincoln's reverence for the church and the worship which its services promote, was shown, while he was President, not alone by his attendance on Sunday but also at the weekly meeting. The late William Henry Roberts, D. D., for so many years Stated Clerk of the General Assembly of the Presbyterian Church in the U. S. A., testifies to that fact in his Foreword to *Abraham Lincoln, The Christian,* by William J. Johnson, under date of November 26, 1912:

"It was my privilege as a young man to have known Abraham Lincoln. Entering the service of the United States government in the fall of 1863, the first Sabbath of my sojourn in Washington City I went to the New York Avenue Presbyterian Church. When the time for the long prayer came, according to immemorial usage in many Presbyterian congregations, a number of the men stood up for prayer, and among those upright figures I noticed in particular that of the President of the United States. As a member of the New York Avenue Church I was seated not far from Mr. Lincoln at Sunday services for a year and a half, and his attitude was always that of an earnest and devout worshipper. He was also an attendant at the weekly meeting, though for a considerable period taking part in the service, privately. It having become known that he was an attendant at the prayer meeting, many persons would gather in or near the church at the close of the service in order to have access to

him for various purposes. Desiring to put an end to
these unwelcome interruptions, the Rev. Dr. Phineas
D. Gurley, the pastor of Mr. Lincoln, arranged to have
the President sit in the pastor's room, the door of
which opened upon the lecture room, and there Mr.
Lincoln would take a silent part in the service. He
informed his pastor on several occasions that he had
received great comfort from the meetings, and for the
reason that they had been characterized more by
prayer than by the making of addresses. . . . .

"It will be fifty years next fall since I came into direct touch with the man, who in the providence of
God was the liberator of a race, and I shall always
hold in sweet and blessed memory my first sight of
him, as a devout worshipper standing for prayer in
the sanctuary of the Most High."

It is gratifying to all lovers of Lincoln that this
beautiful and impressive picture of the Great War
President, in the attitude of a devout worshipper, has
been left us by Dr. Roberts. It adds one more link to
the chain of evidence that Lincoln's soul was filled with
reverence, and it increases the interest which centers
about the historic church where he regularly wor-
shipped and in that way made known his faith in God.

There can be no prayer without reverence and there
is no doubt that Lincoln prayed. Mr. Nicolay, his secretary, who knew him most intimately, says:

"There is not the slightest doubt that he believed in
a Supreme Being of omnipotent power and omniscient
watchfulness over the children of men, and that this
great Being could be reached by prayer. Mr. Lincoln

was a praying man; I know that to be a fact. And I have heard him request people to pray for him, which he would not have done had he not believed that prayer is answered. Many a time have I heard Mr. Lincoln ask ministers and Christian women to pray for him, and he did not do this for effect. He was no hypocrite, and had such reverence for sacred things that he would not trifle with them."

The truth is that he literally talked with God in a simple, direct, familiar way, unknown to mere formalists of the type who "love to pray standing in the synagogues and in the corner of the streets that they may be seen of men." Of the numerous instances which prove that he thus communed with God in prayer, none is more convincing than the one connected with his visit on July 5, 1863, to General Sickles as he lay wounded in the hospital at Washington just after the great victory at Gettysburg. To the truthfulness of this incident, recorded in *Abraham Lincoln, The Christian,* General Sickles certified on February 11, 1911:

"In reply to a question from General Sickles whether or not the President was anxious about the battle at Gettysburg, Lincoln gravely said, 'No, I was not; some of my Cabinet and many others in Washington were, but I had no fears.' General Sickles inquired how this was, and seemed curious about it. Mr. Lincoln hesitated, but finally replied: 'Well, I will tell you how it was. In the pinch of your campaign up there, when everybody seemed panic-stricken, and nobody could tell what was going to happen, oppressed by the gravity of our affairs, I went to my room one

BATTLEFIELD OF GETTYSBURG, WHERE LINCOLN DELIVERED HIS FAMOUS ADDRESS

SAINT-GAUDENS' STATUE OF LINCOLN
This statue is in Lincoln Park, Chicago. A replica stands in London.

day, and I locked the door, and got down on my knees
before Almighty God, and prayed to Him mightily for
victory at Gettysburg. I told Him that this was His
war, and our cause His cause, but we couldn't
stand another Fredericksburg or Chancellorsville.
And I then and there made a solemn vow to Almighty
God, that if He would stand by our boys, at Gettysburg, I would stand by Him. And He *did* stand by
you boys, and I *will* stand by Him. And after that (I
don't know how it was, and I can't explain it), soon a
sweet comfort crept into my soul that God Almighty
had taken the whole business into His own hands and
that things would go all right at Gettysburg. And
that is why I had no fears about you.' "

In view of the reverence which Lincoln always manifested in all the relations of life, it is certainly most
fitting, and perhaps more than a mere coincidence,
that the last act of Congress signed by him was the
one requiring that the motto, so constantly exemplified in his life, "In God We Trust," should thereafter
be inscribed upon all national coin; and that, in the
last address he ever made, April 11, 1865, in referring
to the joy which "the hope of a righteous and speedy
peace" brought, he should say:

"In the midst of this, however, He from whom all
blessings flow must not be forgotten."

CHAPTER III

LINCOLN'S LOYALTY

THE word loyalty is fraught with deep meaning. It is synonomous with faithfulness and devotion to home, to friends, to lawful government, to a righteous cause, and to a just principle.

Loyalty implies moral consistency which is essential to firmness of character. Moral consistency should not be confounded with mere consistency of opinion, which it is reasonable to assume Emerson had in mind in the oft-quoted sentence from his celebrated essay on "Self-Reliance":

"A foolish consistency is the hobgoblin of little minds, adored by little statesmen and philosophers and divines. With consistency a great soul has simply nothing to do. He may as well concern himself with his shadow on the wall. Out upon your guarded lips! Sew them up with packthread, do. Else if you would be a man speak what you think to-day in words as hard as cannon balls, and to-morrow, speak what to-morrow thinks in hard words again, though it contradict everything you said to-day."

While there is some truth in the statement that only fools never change their minds, it is absolutely true that only moral weaklings and moral cowards are devoid of moral consistency. Only those who have unalterable convictions upon the great question of right and wrong are ever able to speak to-day or to-morrow or any time "in words as hard as cannon balls." With consistency of opinion, it is certainly true that "a great soul has simply nothing to do." With moral consistency—loyalty to a righteous cause or to a just principle—a great soul has everything to do.

Lack of such loyalty has been the cause of failure on the part of some otherwise really great men of our nation, who were unable in a moral crisis to stand true to what must have appealed to them as right. Instead they heeded the call of passing expediency rather than the enduring demand of fidelity to duty.

Daniel Webster is an example of such failure. His memorable "Seventh of March (1850) Speech" can be studied with profit as a warning against any attempt to compromise with wrong in order that good may come. Even at this late day, it is impossible to read this speech without a feeling of deep regret that as great a man as Webster lacked the moral consistency to keep himself true to the principles which he had held and courageously defended on so many previous occasions. Whatever his motive may have been, he failed in this speech to remain loyal to the moral convictions on the question of slavery, which had characterized all his words and acts, up to that time. And he paid dearly for the failure. "If the Seventh of March Speech was right," declares Henry Cabot Lodge in his biography of Webster, "then all that had gone before was false and wrong. In that speech he broke from his past, from his own principles and from the principles of New England, and closed his splendid public career with a terrible mistake."

In the speeches of Stephen A. Douglas, another man of rare ability and remarkable power, will be found many evidences of his entire lack of any positive convictions on the great moral question of slavery. In fact he freely admitted and frequently declared in his speeches that he did not care whether slavery was voted up or down. In the senatorial contest of 1858, Douglas, without any convictions on this moral issue, was successful and went to the United States Senate. Lincoln, with positive convictions and the courage to express them, was unsuccessful, but went later to the Presidency and "finally to immortality."

The loyalty of both Webster and Douglas to the Union has never been and never can be questioned. The failure of both was a moral failure, due either to a lack of conviction on the great moral question of their day, or a lack of loyalty to such conviction. Webster died nearly a decade before the opening of the Civil War which ended with the abolition of slavery and the preservation of the Union that he had always defended with all the power of his great eloquence. Douglas lived to see the Union attacked by the friends of slavery, which he had failed to recognize as a moral issue. But in justice to his memory it must not be forgotten that when the crisis came, in the brief remnant of life which remained to him, he was loyal to the Union and to President Lincoln, to whom he pledged his support to sustain him "in the exercise of all his constitutional functions to preserve the Union, and maintain the Government, and defend the Federal capital."

On the monument erected to his memory in the grounds of the State House, Springfield, Illinois, is recorded his dying message to his children:

"Tell them to obey the laws and support the Constitution of the United States."

No better example of loyalty characterized by moral consistency based upon and guided by profound moral conviction can be found than that furnished by the life of Abraham Lincoln. In thought, word, and deed he was guided and controlled in all his actions in relation to slavery by two fundamental principles:

1. Uncompromising opposition to the extension of slavery because it was wrong.

2. Unswerving loyalty to the Constitution of the United States as the Fundamental Law, together with implicit obedience to all laws enacted in accordance with its provisions.

Lincoln always believed that slavery was wrong in both theory and practice. In his remarkable letter to Mr. A. G. Hodges of Frankfort, Kentucky, dated April 4, 1864, he says:

"I am naturally antislavery. If slavery is not wrong, nothing is wrong. I cannot remember when I did not so think and feel."

Verification of this conviction, expressed within a year of the close of Lincoln's life, is found in all his actions relating to slavery. Tradition, at least, asserts that, when a young man on his famous voyage to New Orleans, he was so stirred with the revolting scenes which he witnessed in the slave market of that city that he declared:

"If I ever have a chance at that thing, I'll hit it hard."

Under the historic Ordinance of 1787 freedom from slavery was guaranteed to all the great Northwest Territory. Illinois, one of the states carved from this Territory, was admitted into the Union in 1818. In 1822-23, an attempt was made to change it into a slave state. This attempt was defeated largely through the influence of Governor Coles, a Virginian by birth, but a strong antislavery man, who used all his influence and spent all his four years' salary in the interest of freedom. The bitterness of the pro-slavery sentiment in Illinois, as late as 1837, is shown in the murder of Elijah P. Lovejoy, who published an anti-slavery paper in Alton.

And yet, notwithstanding this condition of affairs, Lincoln's loyalty to his conviction that slavery was wrong led him to record that conviction in the historic "Lincoln-Stone Protest," which was formally entered upon the journal of the legislature of which he was a member, nearly a year before the Alton tragedy. This "Protest" called attention to the fact that resolutions upon the subject of domestic slavery had passed both branches of the General Assembly and declared the belief "that the institution of slavery is founded on both injustice and bad policy." Lincoln was one of only six members of the legislature to vote in the negative on the resolutions against which the "Protest" was recorded, while the "Protest" itself was endorsed by only his colleague, Dan Stone, and himself. Although in a hopeless, and no doubt a very unpopular minority, Lincoln was loyal to his conviction and left no doubt as to his exact position and feeling on the question of slavery. It took rare moral courage for a young man only twenty-eight years of age and just entering upon a political career to stand almost alone for what he believed was right. But Lincoln did not hesitate. Loyalty to both his conscience and his reason would not permit him to keep silent.

When in 1820 the Missouri Compromise became effective, it was vainly hoped that the vexatious slavery question was settled. As late as 1849 and 1850, this Compromise was strongly defended by Senator Douglas, who described it as having had "an origin akin to the Constitution" and as having become "canonized in the hearts of the American people as a sacred thing which no ruthless hand would ever be reckless enough to disturb." In view of this fact, it is not difficult to realize the surprise and indignation which swept over the North, when in 1854, the Missouri Compromise was repealed by the passage of the Kansas-Nebraska Act, largely through the influence of Senator Douglas.

After Lincoln closed his one term in Congress in 1849, he devoted his time and attention to the practice of law. "In 1854," he says, in his *Autobiography*, written in the third person, "this profession had almost superseded the thought of politics in his mind, when the repeal of the Missouri Compromise aroused him as never before."

The contest was on between Douglas, who "didn't care whether slavery was voted up or down," and Lincoln, who believed "that the institution of slavery is founded on both injustice and bad policy." This contest was to continue through the most remarkable campaign in American history and to center about the historic Lincoln-Douglas Debates which stirred the whole nation to its depths.

Preliminary to the regular debates, the two contestants met on different occasions and discussed the great issue of the day. One of the most noted of these meetings was in Peoria, Illinois, on October 16, 1854. In the afternoon of that day Douglas addressed a large audience and announced that Lincoln, who was present, would follow him and that he, in turn, would follow Lincoln. It was after five o'clock when Douglas concluded his address of three hours, and Lincoln was called to the platform. Since he expected to occupy three hours in answering Douglas, who had announced that he would take an hour to reply to Lincoln, it is not surprising that he suggested an adjournment till after supper and that the audience accepted the suggestion and reassembled at seven o'clock. Lincoln's frankness is well illustrated in his statement to the audience to the effect that he had no doubt that they were surprised that he had given to one of such high reputation and known ability as Judge Douglas such an advantage over himself; but that in consenting to it, he was not wholly unselfish, since in so doing he suspected that if it were understood that the Judge's speech was finished, those who favored him would leave, and not hear the reply, adding, with a touch of his rare humor, "But by giving him the close I felt confident you would stay for the fun of hearing him skin me."

With his accurate knowledge of the history of the Missouri Compromise and the steps leading to its repeal, and with his unusual power of critical analysis, Lincoln proceeded to answer Douglas and to picture the ominous effects of the repeal of that Compromise. With his soul on fire with indignation at the wrong and injustice of slavery, and the admitted indifference of Douglas to it, he expressed his own opinions and feelings in the following, quoted from his reply:

"This declared indifference, but, as I must think, covert real zeal for the spread of slavery, I cannot but hate. I hate it because of the monstrous injustice of slavery itself. I hate it because it deprives our republican example of its just influence in the world; enables the enemies of free institutions with plausibility to taunt us as hypocrites; causes the real friends of freedom to doubt our sincerity; and especially because it forces so many good men among ourselves into an open war with the very fundamental principles of civil liberty, criticizing the Declaration of Independence, and insisting that there is no right principle of action but self-interest.

"Slavery is founded in the selfishness of man's nature—opposition to it in his love of justice. These principles are in eternal antagonism, and when brought into collision so fiercely as slavery extension brings them, shocks and throes and convulsions must ceaselessly follow. Repeal the Missouri Compromise, repeal all compromises, repeal the Declaration of Independence, repeal all past history, you still cannot repeal human nature. It still will be the abundance of man's heart that slavery extension is wrong, and out of the abundance of his heart his mouth will continue to speak.

"Little by little, but steadily as man's march to the grave, we have been giving up the old for the new faith. Nearly eighty years ago we began by declaring that all men are created equal; but now from that beginning we have run down to the other declaration, that for some men to enslave others is a 'sacred right of self-government.' These principles cannot stand together. They are as opposite as God and Mammon; and whoever holds to the one must despise the other."

At Bloomington, Illinois, on May 29, 1856, Lincoln made a speech which aroused such interest and enthusiasm that even the newspaper reporters sat spellbound and failed to take notes. However, notes of this speech, commonly referred to as "The Lost Speech," were taken in longhand by Henry C. Whitney, one of the biographers of Lincoln, who, in writing out his notes for publication, claimed to have followed the argument and in many instances to have reproduced the exact statements of Lincoln.

From his report of this speech the following quotation is taken:

"Slavery is a violation of the eternal right. We have temporized with it from the necessities of our condition; but as sure as God reigns and school children read, that black foul lie can never be consecrated into God's hallowed truth!"

"We want and must have," said Lincoln in December, 1859, when making a tour of the Territory of

Kansas, "a national policy as to slavery which deals with it as being wrong. Whoever would prevent slavery becoming national and perpetual yields all when he yields to a policy which treats it as being right, or as a matter of indifference."

In his historic Cooper Institute Speech, February 27, 1860, Lincoln said:

"If slavery is right, all words, acts, laws, and constitutions against it are themselves wrong, and should be silenced and swept away. If it is right, we cannot justly object to its nationality—its universality! If it is wrong, they (the Southern States) cannot justly insist upon its extension—its enlargement. All they ask we could readily grant, if we thought slavery right; all we ask they could as readily grant, if they thought it wrong. Their thinking it right, and our thinking it wrong, is the precise fact upon which depends the whole controversy.

* * * *

"Let us be diverted by none of those sophistical contrivances wherewith we are so industriously plied and belabored—contrivances such as groping for some middle ground between the right and the wrong; vain as the search for a man who should be neither a living man nor a dead man; such as a policy of 'don't care' on a question about which all true men do care; such as Union appeals beseeching true Union men to yield to Disunionists, reversing the divine rule, and calling, not the sinners, but the righteous to repentance; such as invocations to Washington, imploring men to unsay what Washington said and undo what Washington did.

"Neither let us be slandered from our duty by false accusations against us, nor frightened from it by menaces of destruction to the government, nor of dungeons to ourselves. Let us have faith that right makes might; and in that faith let us to the end dare to do our duty as we understand it."

The foregoing expressions regarding slavery furnish conclusive evidence that Lincoln never wavered in his loyalty to the first principle, which guided and controlled all his actions, that of uncompromising opposition to the extension of slavery because it was wrong.

In order that intelligent and just consideration may be given to Lincoln's attitude toward slavery as it existed under the Constitution and the laws enacted in accordance with its provisions, it is necessary to review the salient facts relating to its history; also to keep in mind that the second fundamental principle which controlled his actions, was unswerving loyalty to the Constitution and implicit obedience to law.

Slavery began in the American colonies with the importation of slaves into Virginia in 1619, and was gradually introduced into the other colonies. Being unprofitable in the northern states and not in harmony with the sentiments of a great majority of the people, it was either abolished directly or else indirectly, by gradual emancipation. Being profitable in the southern states, especially after the invention of the cotton gin in 1793, it soon came to be considered a necessity to the industrial life of that section.

When the government of the United States was instituted in 1789 the slave trade was quite general throughout the world. It was favored by the British government during the eighteenth century. The Constitution of the United States, adopted in 1787, forbade Congress to prohibit it until 1808, and gave to the several states representation in the House of Representatives for three-fifths of their slaves. Provision was made for the arrest and return of fugitive slaves, by law of the colonies, in the Ordinance of 1787, and in the Constitution.

In 1793, Congress passed the first Fugitive Slave Act, which provided that upon proof of ownership furnished by the owner before a magistrate of the locality where the slave was found, the magistrate should order the slave delivered up to the owner without a trial by jury. Hindering the arrest or harboring a runaway slave was punishable by a fine of five hundred dollars. Under this act the federal government assumed the responsibility for the pursuit and return of fugitive slaves. In the Compromise of 1850, the new Fugitive Slave Act provided for the trial of cases in a "summary manner" by United States Commissioners, and for a fine of one thousand dollars for the failure of a United States marshal to execute a warrant for the arrest or removal of a fugitive slave. By this act, citizens were required to assist in the execution of the law, when called upon to do so, under penalty of a heavy fine and civil damages to the owner of the slave, together with imprisonment for six months for any assistance given to the fugitive or any attempt to rescue him. The only evidence of ownership required was the affidavit of the person who claimed the slave.

In 1854, the Missouri Compromise was practically repealed by the passage of the Kansas-Nebraska Bill, and in 1857 the whole nation was stirred to its depths by the Dred-Scott Decision, which in substance declared that in the Declaration of Independence and in the Constitution of the United States, negroes were included or referred to only as property and could not become citizens of the United States nor sue in the Federal courts. And further, that under the Constitution neither Congress nor the legislature of a territory had the power to prohibit slavery in any territory of the United States. With these facts in mind it is interesting to study the evidences of Lincoln's loyalty to the Constitution and of his obedience to all constitutionally enacted laws relating to slavery.

In the "Lincoln-Stone Protest," previously referred to, he was loyal not only to his moral conviction that slavery was wrong as indicated by the declaration of his belief "that the institution of slavery is founded upon both injustice and bad policy," but he was also equally loyal to the Constitution as shown by the declaration of his belief "that the Congress of the United States has no power under the Constitution to interfere with the institution of slavery in the different states."

A little more than a decade later, when a member of Congress, Lincoln introduced a carefully framed bill providing for the abolishment of slavery in the District of Columbia. This bill was based upon the idea which, later on when he was President, he frequently urged Congress to adopt and the border slave states to

accept, that "the just and generous mode of getting rid
of the barbarous institution of slavery was by a system
of compensated emancipation, giving freedom to the
slave and a money indemnity to the owner." The provisions of this bill, which never came to a vote, breathe
the same spirit of loyalty to his convictions with respect to both slavery and the Constitution.

Many of the extremely radical opponents of slavery
did not hesitate to denounce the Dred-Scott Decision
in unmeasured terms and to suggest such radical action as accorded with their radical views, regardless
of the Constitution and the laws. Although Lincoln's
keen sense of right and justice was outraged by this
Decision, his loyalty to the Constitution and his reverence for law and order kept him from saying anything of a harsh or revolutionary nature. On June 26,
1857, he replied to a speech made by Senator Douglas,
who had defended the decision of the Supreme Court,
notwithstanding the fact that it completely contra-
dicted his theory of popular sovereignty that the people of a territory could decide the slavery question
for themselves. In this speech, Lincoln said:

"We believe as much as Judge Douglas (perhaps
more) in obedience to, and respect for, the judicial
department of government. We think its decisions
on constitutional questions, when fully settled, should
control, not only the particular cases decided, but the
general policy of the country, subject to be disturbed
only by amendments of the Constitution as provided
in that instrument itself. More than this would be
revolution. But we think the Dred-Scott Decision is
erroneous. We know the court that made it has often

overruled its own decisions, and we shall do what we can to have it overrule this. We offer no resistance to it."

Lincoln's loyalty to the Constitution must have been severely tested by the provision relating to the return of fugitive slaves—a provision which undoubtedly grieved his generous soul, so filled with a hatred of the injustice of slavery. And yet he did not hesitate in his First Inaugural Address to quote this provision and to express his conviction that "All members of Congress swear their support to the whole Constitution—to this provision as much as to any other." The assurance of the sincerity of his own purpose to support the whole Constitution is indicated in his declaration:

"I take the official oath to-day with no mental reservations, and with no purpose to construe the Constitution or laws by any hypercritical rules."

That this oath was, to him, a most sacred one is revealed in his fervid appeal to his "dissatisfied fellow-countrymen":

"You have no oath registered in heaven to destroy the government, while I shall have the most solemn one to 'preserve, protect, and defend it.'"

Because of his unswerving loyalty to the Constitution, he would not perform any act in violation of its provisions, even to interfere with slavery. On this account he was severely criticised by men who should have defended him in his conscientious performance of duty. One of the severest of these unreasoning critics was Horace Greeley, the great editor of the *New York Tribune*, which wielded a mighty influence

LINCOLN AT THE FRONT

This picture shows Lincoln visiting the headquarters of General
McClellan during the last years of the Civil War.

PORTRAIT OF LINCOLN

This autographed picture was presented to Mr. Thomas F. Rochford, of Brooklyn, by Mr. Hagen, a classmate of Lincoln.

on northern public sentiment. Lincoln's historic letter to Greeley, August 22, 1862, will always stand as a fine example of courtesy and generosity in replying to unwarranted and unkindly criticism as well as of candor in outlining the policy which governed in the prosecution of the war. As an example of convincing reasoning and fine diction, it has never been surpassed:

"I have just read yours of the 19th (August, 1862), addressed to me through the *New York Tribune*. If there be in it any statements or assumptions of fact which I may know to be erroneous, I do not, now and here, controvert them. If there be in it any inferences which I may believe to be falsely drawn, I do not, now and here, argue against them. If there be perceptible in it an impatient and dictatorial tone, I waive it in deference to an old friend whose heart I have always supposed to be right.

"As to the policy I 'seem to be pursuing,' as you say, I have not meant to leave any one in doubt.

"I would save the Union. I would save it the shortest way under the Constitution. The sooner the national authority can be restored, the nearer the Union will be 'the Union as it was.' If there be those who would not save the Union unless they could at the same time save slavery, I do not agree with them. If there be those who would not save the Union unless they could at the same time destroy slavery, I do not agree with them. My paramount object in this struggle is to save the Union, and is not either to save or to destroy slavery. If I could save the Union without freeing any slave, I would do it; and if I could save it by freeing all the slaves, I would do it; and if I could save it by freeing some and leaving others alone, I would also do that. What I do about slavery and the colored race, I do because I believe it helps to save the Union; and what I forbear, I forbear because I do not believe it would help to save the Union. I shall do less whenever I shall believe what I am doing hurts the cause, and I shall do more whenever I shall believe doing more will help the cause. I shall try to correct errors when shown to be errors, and I shall adopt new views so fast as they shall appear to be true views.

"I have here stated my purpose according to my view of official duty; and I intend no modification of my oft-expressed personal wish that all men everywhere could be free."

As the war progressed, it became more and more evident that the destruction of slavery would come with the saving of the Union and that its abolition would help to save the Union. The processes through which the mind of Lincoln passed in reaching the conclusion that freeing the slaves would help to restore the national authority are shown in his letter of April 4, 1864, to Mr. A. G. Hodges of Frankfort, Kentucky. This letter presents in the straightforward, logical, and sincere manner, so characteristic of all Lincoln's work and acts, the different steps taken in dealing with slavery, every one of which was in strict accord with his belief that slavery was wrong and in loyal obedience to the solemn oath which he had taken "to preserve, protect, and defend the Union."

This letter is a masterpiece of English and furnishes a striking illustration of Lincoln's loyalty to the two principles which controlled his actions toward slavery:

"You ask me to put in writing the substance of what I verbally said the other day in your presence, to Governor Bramlette and Senator Dixon. It was about as follows:

"'I am naturally antislavery. If slavery is not wrong, nothing is wrong. I cannot remember when I did not so think and feel, and yet I have never understood that the Presidency conferred upon me an unrestricted right to act officially upon this judgment and feeling. It was in the oath I took that I would, to the best of my ability, preserve, protect, and defend the Constitution of the United States. I could not take the office without taking the oath. Nor was it my view that I might take an oath to get power and break the oath in using the power. I understand, too, that in ordinary civil administration this oath even forbade me to practically indulge my primary abstract judgment on the moral question of slavery. I had publicly declared this many times, and in many ways. And I aver that, to this day, I have done no official act in mere deference to my abstract judgment and feeling on slavery.

"'I did understand, however, that my oath to preserve the Constitution to the best of my ability imposed upon me the duty of preserving, by every indispensable means, that government—that nation, of which that Constitution was the organic law. Was it possible to lose the nation and yet preserve the Constitution? By general law, life and limb must be protected, yet often a limb must be amputated to save a life; but a life is never wisely given to save a limb. I felt that measures otherwise unconstitutional might become lawful by becoming indispensable to the preservation of the Constitution through the preservation of the nation. Right or wrong, I assumed this ground, and now avow it. I could not feel that, to the best of my ability, I had even tried to preserve the Constitution, if, to save slavery or any minor matter, I should permit the wreck of government, country and Constitution all together. When, early in the war, General Fremont attempted military emancipation, I forbade it, because I did not then think it an indispensable necessity. When, a little later, General Cameron, then Secretary of War, suggested the arming of the blacks, I objected because I did not yet think it an indispensable necessity. When, still later, General Hunter attempted military emancipation, I again forbade it, because I did not yet think the indispensable necessity had come. When in March and May and July, 1862, I made earnest and successive appeals to the border States to favor compensated emancipation, I believed the indispensable necessity for military emancipation and arming the blacks would come unless averted by that measure. They declined the proposition, and I was, in my best judgment, driven to the alternative of either surrendering the Union, and with it the Constitution, or of laying strong hand upon the colored element. I chose the latter. In choosing it, I hoped for greater gain than loss; but of this, I was not entirely confident. More than a year of trial now shows no loss by it in our foreign relations, none in our home popular sentiment, none in our white military force—no loss by it anyhow or anywhere. On the contrary it shows a gain of quite a hundred and thirty thousand soldiers, seamen, and laborers. These are palpable facts, about which, as facts, there can be no caviling. We have the men; and we could not have had them without the measure.

" 'And now let any Union man who complains of the measure test himself by writing down in one line that he is for subduing the rebellion by force of arms; and in the next, that he is for taking these hundred and

thirty thousand men from the Union side, and placing
them where they would be but for the measure he
condemns. If he cannot face his case so stated, it is
only because he cannot face the truth.

"I add a word which was not in the verbal conversation. In telling this tale I attempt no compliment
to my own sagacity. I claim not to have controlled
events, but confess plainly that events have controlled
me. Now, at the end of three years' struggle, the nation's condition is not what either party, or any man,
devised or expected. God alone can claim it. Whither it is tending seems plain. If God now wills the removal of a great wrong, and wills also that we of the
North, as well as you of the South, shall pay fairly
for our complicity in that wrong, impartial history
will find therein new cause to attest and revere the
justice and goodness of God."

The history of the final act in the great tragedy of
African slavery in the United States can be briefly
told. Having been fully convinced that the "indispensable necessity" for military emancipation had come
and that "measures otherwise unconstitutional" would
be "lawful" because "indispensable to the preservation
of the Constitution through the preservation of the
Union," Lincoln on July 22, 1862, read to his Cabinet
the first draft of the Emancipation Proclamation.
Criticisms and suggestions were offered by different
members of the Cabinet. One suggestion, made by
Secretary Seward, that it be postponed until it could
be given to the country with the support of a military
victory, appealed to Lincoln and he put the Proclamation aside. On September 22, 1862, he informed his
Cabinet that he thought the time had come; that when

the rebel army was at Frederick, he had determined, as soon as it had been driven out of Maryland, he would issue the Proclamation; that he had said nothing to any one, but had promised himself and his Maker that he would issue it; and that he was going to fulfill that promise. This he proceeded to do by issuing the preliminary proclamation of September 22, 1862. On December 30, 1862, he presented to his Cabinet the final draft of the Proclamation. On the following day, the members of the Cabinet again offered their criticisms and suggestions. Lincoln then carefully rewrote it, and on January 1, 1863, the immortal document was published to the world. It quoted the announcement of the preliminary proclamation of September which was issued "as a fit and necessary war measure"; named the states and parts of states which were in rebellion against the United States on that day; ordered and declared "that all persons held as slaves within said designated States and parts of States are, and henceforward shall be free"; and "that such persons of suitable condition will be received into the armed service of the United States." In the closing paragraph, the form of which was submitted by Secretary Chase, Lincoln added after the words, "warranted by the Constitution," the very important qualifying phrase, "upon military necessity"—additional evidence of his loyalty to the Constitution:

"And upon this act, sincerely believed to be an act of justice, warranted by the Constitution upon military necessity, I invoke the considerate judgment of mankind and the gracious favor of Almighty God."

Later on, after the death of the mighty leader who had so directed affairs that slavery, which he had always abhorred, was overthrown and the Union saved, the Constitution which he revered and to which he was always loyal, was so amended as to complete emancipation. Lincoln's loyalty, founded upon convictions which gave to all his acts moral consistency, had won the victory for the right, and slavery, which had been sanctioned by the Constitution and protected by various laws enacted by Congress, was abolished forever from the United States.

CHAPTER IV

LINCOLN'S HONESTY

THAT honesty was one of the dominant traits of Lincoln's character is the universal testimony of all who knew him. It was, as Justice David Davis of the United States Supreme Court, one of Lincoln's life-long friends, declared in his beautiful tribute to his memory, "the framework of his mental and moral being." His honesty constantly manifested itself in all that he said and did. It was the controlling factor in all his activities, including even the sports in which he so often took part.

The great physical strength with which Lincoln was endowed made him, when quite a young man, a recognized leader in the sports which characterized the frontier life of which he was a part. He loved these sports, both for their own sake and for the human companionship which they fostered. His humility, which was such a prominent factor in all the intellectual and political achievements of his later life, kept him from making any idle boasts as to his physical powers. He had neither the desire nor the inclination to pick a quarrel, which he always abhorred; and he rarely, if ever, initiated a physical contest.

Not all of his friends, however, were as modest as he

with reference to his abilities. One of these friends, Denton Offutt, for whom Lincoln worked in various capacities, was loud in his praise. He did not hesitate to declare that "Abe knew more than any man in the United States" and that "he could beat any man in the country, running, jumping or 'wrastling.'" The sweeping statement relative to the knowledge possessed by Abe seems to have aroused little or no excitement in the community. Perhaps the extent of the territory included in this statement was somewhat bewildering to those who heard it and who had no means of disproving it. But to be told that Abe could out-run, out-jump, and "out-wrastle" any man in the country, was the signal for action. Such an announcement could not be permitted to pass unchallenged. The challenge promptly came from the ranks of the "Clary Grove Boys," a crowd of young ruffians who visited New Salem once or twice a week for the purpose of drinking, fighting, or otherwise disturbing the peace. They considered it a part of their duty to initiate all newcomers by means of such ceremony as they chose to appoint. For a time they let Lincoln alone. His reputation for strength was such as to lead them to be cautious in molesting him. But the fulsome praise of Offutt was more than they could stand. A dispute resulted and finally a challenge to a wrestling-match, which Lincoln most reluctantly accepted, because he was opposed to what he called all such "wooling and pulling."

Jack Armstrong, the leader of the gang, was selected to wrestle with Lincoln, and the contest was on in earnest. Jack's uniformly successful experience up to that time had given him great confidence in his physical powers. He fully expected to win another victory, but he was doomed to disappointment. He soon realized that the "tall stranger" was more than a match for him. His friends rushed to his rescue and by every means known to their kind almost succeeded in throwing Lincoln to the ground. With characteristic self-control, he mustered all his strength, overcame the unfair attack made upon him, and soon won the contest. What was of far greater importance, he won the sincere admiration of his antagonist and all his followers, who were ever afterward his loyal friends. And best of all, he had won by the use of honest, straightforward methods, unaided by any of the tricks and deceptions which too often characterized such sports. He had conclusively proved that he was honest and fair even in a wrestling-match held under the most trying conditions.

When Governor Reynolds of Illinois issued his call for volunteers in the Black Hawk War, Lincoln was one of the first to respond. He was promptly elected captain of his company by a large majority. The record shows that three-fourths of the men made known their choice by the informal procedure of walking over to where Lincoln stood, while the remainder "stood by" a man by the name of Kilpatrick, who had considerable prominence in the community. This first official trust came to Lincoln unsought and was greatly appreciated by him. Frequently in his later life he is reported to have said that no subsequent success brought him such unmixed pleasure. The company contained a number of "genteel ruffians" of the type whose confidence Lincoln had won by his action in the wrestling-match with Jack Armstrong. Something of their character is indicated in the reported statement of Lincoln that in reply to one of the first orders he gave, there came the instant response, "Go to the devil, sir!" This response was simply a manifestation of their fun-loving spirit, and was not intended to show any disrespect to their captain, to whom they were devotedly loyal.

One evening an altercation took place between some of the members of Lincoln's company and those of another company from an adjoining county over a camping ground which both had reached about the same time. To avoid what threatened to be a most disgraceful scuffle, Captain Lincoln proposed to Captain Moore of the other company that they settle the dispute by means of a friendly physical contest. Since Captain Moore had no skill in wrestling, the proposal was modified to allow each company to select its strongest representative. As a result, Lincoln and Lorenzo Dow Thompson were put forward to settle the dispute. Captain Moore's brother was selected as referee, and the fun began in the midst of the wildest enthusiasm on the part of the men, who, it is said, wagered all their property, both present and in future prospect, on the outcome.

The referee announced that "two falls in three would decide the match." In the first round Lincoln was fairly thrown. In the second both men went down together. Then followed a dispute which threatened a general fight of a serious nature. This was avoided by a declaration from Lincoln advising his friends to give up their bets, stating as his reason,—"If he has not thrown me fairly, he could." This honest admission ended the contest, Captain Moore and his company taking possession of the disputed territory. It was a rough scene, but not without its redeeming features, the most striking of which was the absolute fairness and honesty of Lincoln, upon whose mind the affair made a lasting impression. There is abundant evidence that, even when he was President, he frequently discussed the experience with his old-time friends. Of one of these friends, he inquired, "Whatever became of our old antagonist, Thompson,—that big, curly-headed fellow who threw me at Rock Island?" To the expression of surprise on the part of this friend that such a question should be asked, Lincoln "playfully remarked that if he knew where he was living, he would give him a post office by way of showing him that he bore him no ill will."

It was in such contests as these that Lincoln demonstrated that whether winning or losing, he could always be generous, fair, and honest. As a result, he won the love and confidence of the neighbors, who insisted that he should preside over all kinds of games and sports. When he became famous, it was the delight of the old residents, who knew him in these early days, to recall their experiences with him. One of these loved to rehearse how he had persuaded Lincoln, much against his own will, to serve as a judge in a horse race and how he had decided with such fairness as to lead the other judge to declare: "Lincoln is the fairest man I ever had to deal with. If Lincoln is in this country when I die, I want him to be my administrator, for he is the only man I ever met with that was wholly and unselfishly honest."

Thus it was that in the midst of that pioneer life— crude in many respects—in which his young manhood was thrown, Lincoln laid the foundation of his future greatness. The corner stone of that foundation was rugged, uncompromising honesty. It is not surprising, therefore, that early in his life, the friends who knew him best and loved him most should give expression to their abiding confidence in his integrity by calling him "Honest Abe."

In all his financial dealings Lincoln was so scrupulously honest as to be considered eccentric by some. When serving as a clerk in Offutt's store, he sold a small bill of goods to a woman, who paid cash for them. After she had gone, he discovered that he had overcharged her six and a quarter cents. As soon as the store was closed in the evening, he walked several miles into the country to return the amount due.

Another time, just as the store was about to be closed, he sold some tea to a belated customer. On opening the store early the next morning, he noticed that he had used a smaller weight than he had intended. Before eating his breakfast, he proceeded to correct the mistake by taking the balance of the order to the customer, who lived a long distance from the store.

For three years, Lincoln served as postmaster at New Salem. The place was very small and the mail so light that he is said to have carried it in his hat at times as he walked about distributing it to the people in the community. Finally the population decreased to such an extent that the office was discontinued. No chance to make final settlement with the Post Office Department came until several years later when an agent called on Lincoln, after he had moved to Springfield, and presented a claim for the balance due. This claim was immediately paid by Lincoln in the coin which had been taken in when he was postmaster, with the remark that he never used any money but his own. He never deviated from this rule. Even after he had acquired an extensive law practice, as soon as a fee was paid for service rendered by the law firm of which he was a member, he insisted upon an immediate division. If both partners were present, each received his share; if either was absent, then his share was wrapped in a piece of paper and laid aside for him with a proper notation fully explaining what it was for.

Because of his self-respect and keen sense of honor, he naturally resented any intimation that he was not strictly honest in all his dealings. This is evident in the following interesting letter written to George Spears:

"At your request, I send you a receipt for the postage on your paper. I am somewhat surprised at your request. I will, however, comply with it. The law requires newspaper postage to be paid in advance, and now that I have waited a full year you choose to wound

my feelings by insinuating that unless you get a receipt
I will probably make you pay it again."

The letter enclosed a receipt "in full for postage on
the *Sangamon Journal* up to the first of July, 1834."

After Lincoln's defeat as a candidate for the legislature, he found himself in a serious situation which
he afterward described in the following statement contained in a short autobiography (written in the third
person) prepared at the request of a friend, to be used
for campaign purposes:

> "He was now without means and out of business, but
> was anxious to remain with his friends, who had treat-
> ed him with so much generosity, especially as he had
> nothing elsewhere to go to. He studied what he should
> do—thought of learning the blacksmith trade—thought
> of trying to study law—rather thought he could not
> succeed at that without a better education."

It was in this crisis that the unfortunate partner-
ship with William F. Berry was formed with the purpose of buying out the store owned by the Herndon
Brothers in New Salem. Later on, the new firm
bought two other stores. For their purchase not a cent
of money was paid, notes being given to cover the
amounts of the different transactions. Berry was dis-
sipated, the business proved to be a disastrous failure,
and was disposed of on credit to the Trent Brothers.
They broke up and left the country. Later, Berry died
and Lincoln became responsible for the entire debt.
With the lax moral ideals relating to business which
prevailed in the community, it would have been easy
for Lincoln to repudiate his liabilities, pleading the

failure of the business and the attendant circumstances. But he did not even try to compromise the
claims against the firm. He deliberately assumed responsibility for the entire amount due and resolutely
determined to keep his promise to the creditors to pay
all as soon as possible. It took him seventeen years to
redeem this promise, but finally every penny of the
debt, which he humorously referred to as "the national
debt," was paid, with interest. While he was serving
in Congress in 1848, portions of his salary were sent
to his law partner from time to time to apply on the
debt.

In writing to an intimate friend of his later years,
Lincoln revealed the seriousness of the burden of this
experience by saying:

> "That debt was the greatest obstacle I have ever met
> in my life. I had no way of speculating, and could not
> earn money except by labor, and to earn by labor eleven
> hundred dollars, besides my living, seemed the work of
> a lifetime. There was, however, but one way. I went
> to the creditors and told them that if they would let me
> alone, I would give them all I could earn over my living,
> as fast as I could earn it."

Out of such a disheartening failure in business,
there came the victory of character growth in the form
of that uncompromising honesty for which Abraham
Lincoln was to be known and honored for all time.

Lincoln's sterling honesty was no doubt largely responsible for his appointment as deputy county surveyor, which came to him in his direst need. The work
thus secured "procured bread, and kept soul and body

LINCOLN READING THE EMANCIPATION PROCLAMATION TO HIS CABINET

Left to right are: Secretaries Stanton and Chase, President Lincoln, Secretaries Welles, Smith, Seward (seated), Blair, and Bates

STATUE—LINCOLN AND THE SLAVE

The original of this statue, by Thomas Ball, is in Boston, and the replica is in Washington. It is considered one of the best treatments of the emancipation of the slave.

together," to quote his own words in referring to the matter in after years. The fact that the county surveyor, John Calhoun, who made the choice, was a leading Democrat, while Lincoln was an ardent Whig, gives special significance to this appointment which was made at a time when party spirit ran high and political contests were noted for their bitterness. Striking evidence of the honesty in politics, which was to be such a marked feature in his political career, was shown in his statement made when he was offered the much-needed position. He stated that he would take the office if he could be perfectly free in his political actions but that if his political sentiments or even the expression of them were to be abridged in any way, he would not have it or any other office.

But honesty was not the only qualification which appealed to Calhoun in selecting his deputy. He must have had unlimited faith in Lincoln's ability to prepare to fill the important position to which he had appointed him, for he certainly knew that he had little or no knowledge of surveying. There is a well authenticated tradition at least that when he gave him the appointment he supplied him with the necessary books to study in preparation for his work. Certain it is that in a few weeks Lincoln had prepared himself to enter upon his duties, which were performed with satisfaction to all concerned. He soon became an excellent surveyor, so noted for his accuracy that when disputes arose about corner stones or boundaries, it was not uncommon for the parties to the dispute to agree to send for Lincoln and let him decide the matter.

Lincoln's work as surveyor necessitated the purchase of a horse. He was unable to pay cash and agreed to make settlement on the installment plan. When all but ten dollars had been paid, he was sued for that amount. He was able to raise the money and soon settled this suit. A little later he was sued again on one of the Berry-Lincoln notes. Judgment was obtained and his horse, saddle, and surveying instruments were attached to secure the claim. Loyal friends, who had confidence in his honesty, came to his rescue, redeemed the property, and thus enabled him to continue his work.

Additional evidence of Lincoln's honesty is found in the fact that he never used the information gained as surveyor to make money for himself by means of real estate deals of any kind. No doubt many opportunities for profitable speculation came to him, but he would not use for private gain the knowledge secured in public office, which was to him indeed a public trust, never to be violated in the least particular. His high ideals relative to public office were exemplified many times when he was President. On one occasion, he was strongly urged by a delegation of friends to appoint to an important office one of his closest personal friends. This he declined to do, with the explanation that he did not "regard it as just to the public to pay the debts of personal friendship with offices that belonged to the people."

While serving as postmaster and surveyor, Lincoln rapidly extended his acquaintance. His generous nature, manifested by his readiness to help others, and his gratitude for every favor received, soon turned acquaintance into lasting friendship. His honesty in financial matters won the confidence of all. As a result, he grew in political influence to such an extent that he won four successive victories as a candidate for the legislature, notwithstanding the handicap of his debts. Fortunately, in those days election expenses were not so large as at present. As an indication of this, as well as an illustration of Lincoln's honesty, it is especially interesting to note an incident of one of his campaigns as related by his friend, Joshua Speed.

The Whigs raised two hundred dollars which Speed gave to Lincoln to pay his personal expenses in the campaign. After the election was over, he gave back one hundred and ninety-nine dollars and twenty-five cents of the amount, with the request that it be returned to the subscribers, accompanying the request with the frank statement:

> "I did not need the money. I made the canvass on my own horse; my entertainment, being at the houses of friends, cost me nothing; and my only outlay was seventy-five cents for a barrel of cider, which some farm hands insisted I should treat them to."

In securing the removal of the state capital from Vandalia to Springfield, Lincoln played the leading part. The change was bitterly contested. To secure the removal, the customary trading of votes was undoubtedly indulged in. In playing the political game Lincoln was an expert so long as it was played honestly. But in this contest, as in all others in which he had a part, he never violated his high ideals of right and duty. He was honest from principle and not from policy. He would not use wrong means to secure right ends. An illustration of this is found in his refusal to lend his influence in support of a proposed measure of doubtful character, which his friends urged upon him as a means of helping to win in the contest. It is related that at different conferences, the strongest influences were used without avail. Every possible argument in favor of the proposed measure was presented. Lincoln was implored to lay aside his "inconvenient scruples" and to join in making sure of the removal of the capital. The discussion was brought to a close by Lincoln in what is reported to have been a "most eloquent and powerful" speech against the measure, closing with the frequently quoted words:

> "You may burn my body to ashes and scatter them to the winds of heaven; you may drag my soul down to the regions of darkness and despair, to be tormented forever; but you will never get me to support a measure which I believe to be wrong, although by doing so I may accomplish that which I believe to be the right."

One of the provisions of the act for the removal of the capital was that the place selected should be required to obligate itself to contribute fifty thousand dollars to be used in helping to erect a state house. This was a large sum of money for the citizens of a small frontier town to raise, especially under the financial conditions existing at that time. Stephen A. Douglas, the Register of the Land Office, proposed a measure to release Springfield from the obligation which it was in honor bound to meet. This measure

Lincoln opposed and helped to defeat. His reason for so doing was tersely stated: "We have the benefit; let us stand to our obligation like men."

Under his leadership, the obligation was met, and the honor of the community was maintained by the payment of the full amount in three equal installments. Money for the first two was raised with much difficulty. The last was paid by borrowing the amount from the State Bank, for which a note was given, signed by all the citizens of the town, including Lincoln. For many years this liquidated note was exhibited in one of the banking houses of Springfield—a silent witness to the honesty of the people who followed the advice of Lincoln and stood by their obligation like men.

Many additional instances could be given to show that Lincoln never deviated in his loyalty to the highest ideals of honor and honesty in public as well as in private life. Any proposal to repudiate in the slightest degree a debt or a promise, invariably met with his disapproval. His word was indeed as good as his bond.

In "Notes for a Law Lecture" prepared by Lincoln in 1850 can be found a clear presentation of the high ideals which he always maintained in the practice of law, together with the principles which always guided him in that practice. In this, as in all other relations of life, honesty was the foundation of all his acts. "There is a vague popular belief," says he in these "Notes," "that lawyers are necessarily dishonest. I say vague, because when we consider to what extent confidence and honors are reposed in and conferred upon lawyers by the people, it appears improbable that their impression of dishonesty is very distinct and vivid. Yet the impression is common, almost universal. Let no young man choosing the law for a calling for a moment yield to the popular belief—resolve to be honest, at all events; and if in your own judgment you cannot be an honest lawyer, resolve to be honest without being a lawyer. Choose some other occupation, rather than one in the choosing of which you do, in advance, consent to be a knave."

This advice—"Resolve to be honest at all events," —Lincoln followed in all his relations with his clients, with his associates in the profession, and with the courts. Evidence of this is found both in the tributes paid to him by other members of the bar, who travelled the circuit with him, and in numerous incidents recorded by his biographers.

"But it was morally impossible for Lincoln to argue dishonestly," says Henry C. Whitney, one of his most intimate associates. "He could no more do it than he could steal; it was the same thing to him, in essence, to despoil a man of his property by larceny, or by illogical or flagitious reasoning; and even to defeat a suitor by technicalities or by merely arbitrary law savored strongly of dishonesty by him." . . . "He gave but the slightest attention to rules of evidence, and rarely objected to the admission of anything at all allowable; he could not endure those illiberal practices required at the hands of the complete lawyer; he could not practice or countenance that selfishness which the requirements of good practice demanded. All the generalizations of his mind tended to frankness, fairness, and the attainment of substantial justice, and the simplest mode was to him the best. In entering upon a trial, he stated the whole case on both sides, as he understood it, with fairness and frankness, not attempting to gloss over the faults and imperfections of his own case, or to improperly disparage the adverse side."

In illustration of Lincoln's readiness to admit "anything at all allowable" in the way of evidence, Whitney relates the following personal experience:

"When I was new to the bar, I was trying to keep some evidence out, and was getting along very well with the court, when Lincoln sung out: 'I reckon it would be fair to let that in.' It sounded treasonable, but I had to get used to this eccentricity."

Whitney was not the only member of the bar who was rebuked for an attempt to indulge in sharp practice in order to win a point. His law partner, William H. Herndon, in his life of Lincoln, tells of his experience in running counter to Lincoln's uncompromising honesty:

"Messrs. Stuart and Edwards once brought a suit against a client of ours which involved the title to considerable property. At that time we had only two or three terms of court, and the docket was somewhat crowded. The plaintiff's attorneys were pressing us for a trial, and we were equally as anxious to ward it off. What we wanted were time and a continuance to the next term. We dared not make an affidavit for continuance, founded on facts, because no such pertinent and material facts as the law contemplated existed. Our case for the time seemed hopeless. One morning, however, I accidentally overheard a remark from Stuart indicating his fear lest a certain fact should happen to come into our possession. I felt some relief, and at once drew up a fictitious plea, averring as best I could the substance of the doubts I knew existed in Stuart's mind. The plea was as skilfully drawn as I knew how, and was framed as if we had the evidence to sustain it. The whole thing was a sham, but so constructed as to work the desired continuance, because I knew that Stuart and Edwards believed the facts were as I pleaded them. This was done in the absence and without the knowledge of Lincoln. The plea could not be demurred to, and the opposing counsel dared not take the issue on it. It perplexed them sorely. At length, before further steps were taken, Lincoln came into court. He looked carefully over all the papers in the case, as was his custom, and seeing my ingenious subterfuge, asked, 'Is this seventh plea a good one?' Proud of the exhibition of my skill, I answered that it was. 'But,' he inquired, incredulously, 'is it founded on fact?' I was obliged to respond in the negative, at the same time following up my answer with an explanation of what I had overheard Stuart intimate, and of how these alleged facts could be called facts if a certain construction were put upon them. I insisted that our position was justifiable, and that our client must have time or be ruined. I could see at once it failed to strike Lincoln as just right. He scratched his head thoughtfully and asked, 'Hadn't we better withdraw that plea?

You know it's a sham, and a sham is very often but another name for a lie. Don't let it go on record. The cursed thing may come staring us in the face long after this suit has been forgotten.' The plea was withdrawn. By some agency—not our own—the case was continued and our client's interests were saved. . . . . I venture the assertion that he was the only member of the bar in Springfield who would have taken such a conscientious view of the matter."

"Discourage litigation," advised Lincoln in his "Notes for Law Lectures" previously quoted from. "Persuade your neighbors to compromise whenever you can. Point out to them how the nominal winner is often the real loser—in fees, expenses, and waste of time. As a peacemaker the lawyer has a superior opportunity of being a good man. There will still be business enough.

"Never stir up litigation. A worse man can scarcely be found than one who does this. Who can be more nearly a fiend than he who habitually overhauls the register of deeds in search of defects in titles, whereon to stir up strife, and put money in his pocket? A moral tone ought to be infused into the profession which should drive such men out of it.

"The matter of fees is important, far beyond the mere question of bread and butter involved. Properly attended to, fuller justice is done to both lawyer and client. An exorbitant fee should never be claimed. As a general rule, never take your whole fee in advance, nor any more than a small retainer. When fully paid beforehand, you are more than a common mortal if you can feel the same interest in the case, as if something was still in prospect for you, as well as for your client. And when you lack interest in the case, the job will very likely lack skill and diligence in the performance."

The following incidents conclusively prove that Lincoln followed his own advice to the letter.

To one man who presented a case for consideration, he said:

"Yes, we can doubtless gain your case for you; we can set a whole neighborhood at loggerheads; we can distress a widowed mother and her six fatherless children and thereby get for you six hundred dollars to which you seem to have a legal claim, but which rightly belongs, it appears to me, as much to the woman and children as it does to you. You must remember that some things legally right are not morally right. We shall not take your case, but will give you a little advice for which we will charge you nothing. You seem to be a sprightly, energetic man; we would advise you to try your hand at making six hundred dollars in some other way."

To another client, he wrote:

"I do not think there is the least use of doing anything more with your lawsuit. I not only do not think you are sure to gain it, but I do think you are sure to lose it. Therefore the sooner it ends the better."

In one instance a client, who was a widow, employed Lincoln and Herndon to investigate the title to a valuable piece of property which she owned, with the purpose of determining the validity of certain alleged tax liens against it. The investigation revealed an unsatisfactory description in one of the deeds. To determine the facts in the case, Lincoln surveyed the ground and thereby discovered that a former owner, Charles Matheney, by name, in selling the property, had given a deed for more land than he was paid for, because of

an error in the description. Lincoln decided that this
loss should be made up to the Matheney heirs and so
advised his client, who strenuously objected to following his advice. However, upon learning that unless
she did so, the firm of which Lincoln was a member
would drop the case, the required sum to make resti-
tution was paid, and distributed by Lincoln to the various heirs.

Lincoln's fees for services rendered were exceedingly small—provokingly small to many of his associates at the bar. In some instances, he returned all
the retaining fee given him, when convinced by investigation that the case which he was retained to prosecute or to defend was without merit. A notable illustration of this is related by Carpenter in his *Six
Months at the White House:*

"About the time Mr. Lincoln began to be known as
a successful lawyer, he was waited upon by a lady who
held a real-estate claim which she desired to have him
prosecute,—putting into his hands, with the necessary
papers, a check for two hundred and fifty dollars, as
a retaining fee. Mr. Lincoln said he would look the
case over, and asked her to call again the next day.
Upon presenting herself, Mr. Lincoln told her that he
had gone through the papers very carefully, and he
must tell her frankly that there was not a 'peg' to hang
her claim upon, and he could not conscientiously advise her to bring an action. The lady was satisfied,
and, thanking him, rose to go. 'Wait,' said Mr. Lincoln, fumbling in his vest pocket; 'here is the check you
left with me.' 'But, Mr. Lincoln,' returned the lady,

'I think you have earned *that*.' 'No, no,' he responded, handing it back to her; 'that would not be right. I can't take *pay* for doing my duty.' "

At one time Lincoln prepared a lease for a client, who sent him a check for twenty-five dollars, which he considered a proper charge for the service he had received. In a short time he was surprised to receive the following letter:

> "I have just received yours of the 16th, with check on Flagg and Savage for twenty-five dollars. You must think I am a high-priced man. You are too liberal with your money. Fifteen dollars is enough for the job. I send you a receipt for fifteen dollars, and return to you a ten dollar bill."

On another occasion Ward H. Lamon, Lincoln's associate on the circuit, was retained in an important case by a client named Scott. This client was acting as the guardian of a demented sister, whose property amounting to ten thousand dollars had induced an unprincipled adventurer to attempt to marry the unfortunate girl. In order to carry out his nefarious design, it was necessary to remove the guardian. To oppose this action, Lamon was retained by Scott, who insisted that the amount of the fee be named in advance. Lamon advised against this, as the probabilities were that the matter would be easily settled and the fee would be small. His advice was ignored, and upon the further insistence of Scott, the fee was fixed at two hundred and fifty dollars. This amount was eagerly agreed to by him, in view of what he believed would be a prolonged contest in the court.

Lincoln, himself, took charge of the case when it
came on, and in a few minutes won a complete victory
for his client, who gladly paid to Lamon the promised
fee. When Lincoln learned that the fee was two hundred and fifty dollars, he indignantly exclaimed:
"Lamon, that is all wrong. The service was not worth
that sum. Give him back at least half of it."

In reply to this demand, Lamon protested that the
fee had been agreed upon in advance and that their
client was perfectly satisfied. But Lincoln was im-
movable, as he always was when his ideals of honesty
and justice were at stake. He replied: "That may
be, but I am not satisfied. This is positively wrong.
Go, call him back, and return half the money at least,
or I will not receive one cent of it for my share."

It is, perhaps, needless to add that there was no
further argument. Lincoln's demand was complied
with by returning half of the fee.

It is related that the presiding judge on this occasion, David Davis, afterward a member of the Supreme
Court of the United States by Lincoln's appointment,
took advantage of the situation to rebuke Lincoln by
saying: "I have been watching you and Lamon. You
are impoverishing this bar by your picayune charges
of fees, and the lawyers have reason to complain of
you. You are now almost as poor as Lazarus, and if
you don't make people pay you more for your services,
you will die as poor as Job's turkey."

It is further related that the members of the bar
who overheard the rebuke, said to have been spoken
"in a poorly controlled whisper, which could be heard

throughout the court room," enthusiastically applauded the remarks of the judge and that Lincoln defended his course by saying: "That money comes out of the pocket of a poor, demented girl, and I would rather starve than swindle her in this manner."

It is possible that Judge Davis may have recalled this scene when, shortly after Lincoln's death, he paid tribute to his honesty, as quoted in the opening paragraph of this chapter, and described how he exemplified this honesty in actual practice as follows:

"To his honor be it said that he never took from a client, even when his cause was gained, more than he thought the services were worth and the client could reasonably afford to pay. The people where he practiced law were not rich, and his charges were always small. When he was elected President, I question whether there was a lawyer in the circuit who had been at the bar so long a time, whose means were not larger. It did not seem to be one of the purposes of his life to accumulate a fortune. In fact, outside of his profession, he had no knowledge of the way to make money, and he never even attempted it."

Lincoln's life began in the midst of poverty; much of it was burdened with debt; it ended without the accumulation of a large fortune. But he bequeathed to the world a legacy of honesty and integrity in all that he thought, said, and did in all the varied activities of his marvelous career, that cannot be measured by any material standard—a legacy which will continue to enrich human life as long as time endures.

CHAPTER V

LINCOLN'S SIMPLICITY

WITH Humility, Reverence, Loyalty, and Honesty as the foundation of Lincoln's character, it is not surprising that Simplicity was a distinctive feature of his habits and actions, as well as of his thought and language. All of these were in harmony with the severe simplicity which characterized the society in which he grew up and which has furnished the theme of many writers of both history and fiction.

Interesting and illuminating glimpses of this society are given in the Nicolay and Hay *Life of Lincoln*. In Volume 1, Chapter II, on Indiana, we read:

"Their houses were usually of one room, built of round logs with the bark on. . . . . . Their dress was still mostly of tanned deer-hide, a material to the last degree uncomfortable when the wearer was caught in a shower. Their shoes were of the same, and a good Western authority calls a wet moccasin 'a decent way of going barefoot.' About the time, however, when Lincoln grew to manhood, garments of wool and of tow began to be worn, dyed with the juice of the butternut or white walnut, and the hides of neat-cattle began to be tanned. But for a good while it was only the women who indulged in these novelties. There was little public worship. Occasionally an itinerant preacher visited a county, and the settlers for miles around would go nearly in mass to the meeting. If a man was possessed of a wagon, the family rode luxuriously; but as a rule the men walked and the women went on horseback with the little children in their arms. It was considered no violation of the sanctities of the occasion to carry a rifle and take advantage of any game which might be stirring during the long walk."

"Governor Reynolds," we learn from Chapter III on Illinois, of the same volume, "tells us of a preacher in Sangamon County, who, before his sermon, had set a wolf-trap in view from his pulpit. In the midst of his exhortations his keen eyes saw the distant trap collapse, and he continued in the same intonation with which he had been preaching, 'Mind the text, brethren, till I go kill that wolf!' . . . . . There was very little social intercourse; a visit was a serious matter, involving the expenditure of days of travel. It was the custom among families, when the longing for the sight of kindred faces was too strong to withstand, to move in a body to the distant settlement where their relatives lived and remain with them for months at a time. The claims of consanguinity were more regarded than now. Almost the only festivities were those that accompanied weddings, and these were, of course, of a primitive kind. The perils and adventures through which the young pioneers went to obtain their brides furnish forth thousands of tales by Western firesides. . . . . . . An old farmer of Sangamon

County still talks of a feather-bed weighing fifty-four pounds with which his wife made him swim six rivers under penalty of desertion."

In no way does Lincoln's greatness manifest itself more conclusively than in his actions after he had been elevated to exalted position. Had he possessed littleness of mind or soul, it would have shown itself by acting as if he were ashamed of the simplicity of the life through which he had advanced to prominence and of the friends whose support had made his advancement possible. Had he not been great in thought and action, he might have felt that his election to the Presidency would necessitate a change in the simple manner and habits which had always characterized his life. All of his biographers unite in testifying that, in accepting the nomination to the Presidency, in the campaign which resulted in his election, and in the performance of his official duties as President, he remained unchanged.

At the time of Lincoln's nomination, simplicity characterized the procedure of political conventions. The two prominent candidates for nomination by the Republican party in 1860 were Seward and Lincoln. The name of the former was presented to the convention by William M. Evarts of New York, who simply stated —"I take the liberty to name as a candidate to be nominated by this convention for the office of President of the United States, William H. Seward." Norman B. Judd of Illinois followed with the announcement—"I desire on behalf of the delegation from Illinois, to put in nomination as a candidate for President of the United States, Abraham Lincoln of Illinois."

The people of Springfield, who were in close touch with Lincoln at the time of the convention, have never agreed as to the details of his actions when the news of his nomination reached the city. There is general agreement, however, that he was restless under the strain of anxiety which naturally accompanied the telegraphic reports of the proceedings of the convention; that while he felt that he had a fighting chance of winning, he was not at all confident of success; and that when he was handed the telegram informing him that he had been nominated for the high office of President of the United States, and was surrounded by his neighbors and friends who were rejoicing over the victory, his simplicity found expression in the statement—"My friends, I am glad to receive your congratulations, and as there is a little woman down on Eighth Street who will be glad to hear the news, you must excuse me until I inform her."

The committee which came to Springfield, after the adjournment of the convention, to notify Lincoln of his nomination, was composed of some of the most distinguished men of the nation. When they visited his modest home, noted the simplicity of the surroundings, and watched with keen interest his sad face as he listened to the formal notification of his nomination, which called him to leadership in such a grave crisis, it is not surprising to learn that their hearts were at first filled with misgivings and forebodings. What they thought and how they felt when, in violation of the common custom at that time of serving wine on all such occasions, water was substituted, will probably never be fully realized. However, when they listened to his brief reply phrased in simple but perfect English, expressing his thanks for the honor conferred, together with a full realization of the responsibility which came with the honor, all of the members of the notification committee were satisfied that no mistake had been made in choosing a leader. And whatever their views were on the temperance question, they could not but respect and admire the consistency of a man who would not sacrifice principle to conform to custom.

His formal response in writing followed a few days later:

"SPRINGFIELD, ILL., May 23, 1860

"*Hon. George Ashmun,*

"*President of the Republican National Convention*

"SIR: I accept the nomination tendered me by the Convention over which you presided, and of which I am formally apprised in the letter of yourself and others, acting as a committee of the convention for that purpose.

"The declaration of principles and sentiments which accompanies your letter meets my approval; and it shall be my care not to violate or disregard it in any part.

"Imploring the assistance of Divine Providence, and with due regard to the views and feelings of all who were represented in the convention;—to the rights of all the States, and Territories, and people of the nation; to the inviolability of the Constitution; and the perpetual union, harmony, and prosperity of all—I am

most happy to co-operate for the practical success of
the principles declared by the convention.

> "Your obliged friend and fellow-citizen,
>
> "A. LINCOLN."

The brevity and simplicity of this important letter,
so characteristic of all that Lincoln wrote, were the
result of the most painstaking thought and care in its
preparation. After it was finished, he took it to his
friend, Newton Bateman, State Superintendent of Public Instruction for Illinois, and requested him "to see
if it was all right," remarking that he was "not very
strong on grammar" and "wouldn't like to have any
mistake in it." Only one change was suggested. In
the last clause of the second paragraph, Lincoln had
"split an infinitive" in writing "and it shall be my care
to not violate or disregard it in any part." He was
advised to change the order of the words so as to conform to a rule of grammar considered more essential
to correct usage at that time than at present. This
advice Lincoln followed by making the change, accompanied by the comment, "So you think I better put
those two little fellows end to end, do you?"

The familiar signature to this letter of acceptance,
"A. Lincoln," evidently led to correspondence relative
to his first name, as indicated by the following letter:

> "SPRINGFIELD, ILL., June 4, 1860
>
> "Hon. George Ashmun,
>
> "MY DEAR SIR:
>
> "It seems as if the question whether my first name is
> 'Abraham' or 'Abram' will never be settled. It is 'Abraham,' and if the letter of acceptance is not yet in print,

you may, if you think fit, have my signature thereto
printed 'Abraham Lincoln.'   Exercise your judgment
about this.

"Yours as ever,
                "A. LINCOLN."

This letter furnishes additional evidence of the delightful informality and simplicity which were so
prominent in all of the varied activities of his life.

Interesting glimpses of the unchanged simplicity of
Lincoln's life, after the recognition which made him a
world figure came to him, are given by all his leading
biographers.   In describing the progress of the campaign which resulted in his election to the Presidency,
Miss Tarbell in her *Life of Lincoln* says:

"From May until November this work for the ticket
went on steadily and ardently.   Mr. Lincoln during
all this time remained quietly in Springfield.   The conspicuous position in which he was placed made almost
no difference in his simple life.   He was the same
genial, accessible, modest man as ever, his habits as
unpretentious, his friendliness as great.   The chief
outward change in his daily round was merely one of
quarters.   It seemed to his friends that neither his
home nor his dingy law office was an appropriate place
in which to receive his visitors and they arranged that
a room in the State House which stood on the village
green in the center of the town, be put at his disposal.
He came down to this office every morning about eight
o'clock, always stopping on his way in his old cordial
fashion to ask the news or exchange a story when he
met an acquaintance.   Frequently he went to the post

office himself before going to his office, and came out, his arms loaded with letters and papers.

"He had no regular hours for visitors; there was no ceremony for admittance to his presence. People came when they would. Usually they found the door open; if it was not, it was Mr. Lincoln's own voice which answered 'come in,' to their knock.

* * * * *

"Among his daily visitors there were usually men of eminence from North and South. He received them all with perfect simplicity and always, even on his busiest days, found a moment to turn away from them to greet old friends who had known him when he kept grocery in New Salem or acted as deputy-surveyor of Sangamon County. One day as he talked to a company of distinguished strangers an old lady in a big sun-bonnet, heavy boots and short skirts, walked into the office. She carried a package wrapped in brown paper and tied with a white string. As soon as Mr. Lincoln saw her he left the group, went to meet her and, shaking her hand cordially, inquired for her 'folks.' After a moment the old lady opened her package and taking out a pair of coarse wool socks, she handed them to him. 'I wanted to give you somethin', Mr. Linkin,' she said, 'to take to Washington, and that's all I hed. I spun that yarn and knit them socks myself.' Thanking her warmly, Mr. Lincoln took the socks and holding them up by the toes, one in each hand, he turned to the astonished celebrities and said in a voice full of kindly amusement, 'The lady got my latitude and longitude about right, didn't she, gentlemen?' "

In the Nicolay and Hay *Life of Lincoln,* we learn in the interesting chapter on "The President-Elect" that:

"To all appearances Lincoln remained unchanged. In the unpretending two-story frame house which constituted his home, his daily routine continued as before, except that his door was oftener opened to welcome the curious visitor or to shelter the confidential discussion of ominous occurrences in national affairs. His daily public occupation was to proceed to the Governor's office in the State House, to receive the cordial and entirely unceremonious greetings of high and low,—whosoever chose to enter the open door,— and in the interim to keep himself informed, by means of the daily-increasing budget of letters and newspapers, of the events of the country at large, and to give directions to his private secretary as to what replies should be made to important communications. Beyond the arrival of distinguished visitors, there was in all this no sign of elevation and rulership; he was still the kind neighbor and genial companion, who had for every one he met the same bearing which for a quarter of a century had made his name a household synonym of manly affection, virtue, and honor."

For a few days before leaving Springfield for Washington, the Lincoln family lived at the Chenery House, the leading hotel in the city at that time. From the *Springfield Register,* quoted in Weik's *The Real Lin-*

coln, the following paragraph is taken as a further illustration of Lincoln's simplicity:

"During Mr. Lincoln's sojourn at the hotel he had been visited by many men of prominence whom he had summoned for conferences on national affairs. The complete absence of ostentation and his physical self-reliance was illustrated on the morning of his departure when in the hotel office he roped his trunks with his own hands, took some of the hotel cards, on the back of which he wrote

'A. Lincoln,
White House,
Washington, D. C.'

and tacked them on the trunks, supplementing the act by writing his autograph on another card and giving it to the landlord's daughter."

"Because he did not appoint a goodly portion of his early associates to comfortable offices, and did not interest himself in the welfare of every one whom he had known in Illinois, or met while on the circuit, the erroneous impression grew that his elevation had turned his head," says Herndon, his law partner and biographer, who answered the false accusation by declaring:

"There was no foundation for such an unwarranted conclusion. Lincoln had not changed a particle. He was overrun with duties and weighted down with cares; his surroundings were different and his friends were new, but he himself was the same calm, just, and devoted friend as of yore."

In his meetings with his Cabinet, Lincoln's simplicity was always in evidence. "The Cabinet sessions were absolutely informal," writes Helen Nicolay in *Personal Traits of Abraham Lincoln*. "Regular meetings were held at noon on Tuesdays and Fridays. When special meetings were necessary, the President or Secretary of State called the members together. There was a long table in the Cabinet room, but it was not used as a council board. The President generally stood up and walked about. The others came in and took their seats according to convenience, staying through the session, or stating their business and departing, as pressure of work demanded. Sometimes the meeting was opened by a remark or an anecdote by the President, oftener by the relation of some official or personal happening to one of his advisers."

A characteristic call for a special Cabinet meeting illustrative of the informality described in the preceding paragraph, quoted from the same source, is found in the following:

"Please come to Cabinet ½ past ten to-day.

"A. Lincoln."

But it was not alone in his associations with men and women of all classes and conditions that Lincoln's simplicity was shown. It was revealed in a most striking and beautiful manner by his attitude toward children. He loved his own children with passionate devotion. He was never too busy with the affairs of state to listen to the appeals of little Tad, as his boy Thomas was called, whose unexpected presence caused a break in more than one Cabinet meeting. It is significant that when Lincoln's last picture was taken on April 9, 1865—the day of the surrender at Appomattox, the photographer found the great President and the indulgent father engaged in sharpening a pencil for Tad. One of the most touching tributes to Lincoln's memory is found in the little volume entitled *Tad and His Father*, by F. Lauriston Bullard, in which is recorded a sympathetic account of the many amusing escapades of the little lad whose mischievous pranks often helped to relieve his father's terrible anxiety.

Not infrequently the President would join in "having a little fun with the boys" by playing simple games with Tad and his companions. Sometimes Tad would steal into his father's room late at night, creep into his bed, and thus "the lonely man who bore in his heart the sorrows of the nation and the lad in whose comradeship he found relief from the awful ordeal which it was his duty to endure, the father and the boy together entered the peaceful refuge of sleep."

But Lincoln's generous treatment of children was not by any means confined to his own. He was never happier than when performing some simple acts of kindness for any child anywhere. To Mrs. Mary Edwards Brown of Springfield, Illinois, we are indebted for a most interesting incident in which her mother, a niece of Mrs. Lincoln's, was the recipient of his kindness, when a little girl. She was about to leave her home to take her first trip on a train, to which she had been looking forward with eager anticipation for weeks. It was nearly train time and the drayman had not come for her trunk. She was nervous with fear that she would miss the train and was crying bitterly, when her "Uncle Abe" came by on the way to his office. Learning the cause of her grief, he proceeded at once to quiet her fears by shouldering her trunk and carrying it to the station, while his grateful niece trotted on behind. They reached the station in good time, and the future President of the United States, happy in the knowledge that he had relieved the distress of a child, put her on the train, kissed her good-by, and told her to have a good time.

One of the most interesting incidents connected with the life of Lincoln occurred in his first campaign for the Presidency in 1860, and centered about a little girl who had never seen him, but who was so deeply interested in his success that she wrote him a letter. This letter contained no reference to any of the issues of the campaign. It was written with the purpose of telling him how she thought he could improve his personal appearance.

Descriptions of how this historic letter came to be sent have been given at different times by its writer. Perhaps the most complete of these descriptions is contained in her letter, dated April 3, 1905, and exhibited in the museum connected with the Lincoln monument at Springfield. Permission to quote this letter has been generously granted by Mr. H. W. Fay, the custodian of the Lincoln Tomb:

"I am in receipt of your letter of recent date asking an 'account of the circumstances leading up to Mr. Lincoln's departure from the clean shaven face.' At that time I was a child of less than twelve years of age and was full of interest in the stirring events of the day. Naturally, my father being a Republican, I was, with him, a sincere admirer of Mr. Lincoln, listening to the stories of his early life, his struggles to obtain an education—and deploring the poverty and privation which had so beset his youth, and deeply resenting the slurs cast upon him as being ugly and uncouth in appearance. Perhaps it had so happened that I had not noticed very particularly the cuts of his face which were in the papers, for certainly a glance at the huge and gaudy posters brought us children by our father was rather disappointing, and quick in my desire to improve him, I suggested in a letter that he would look better if he would let his whiskers grow and asked him to let me know if he would, or if he had no time to reply, to let his little girl do so for him.

"I promised him I would do my best to win over two brothers who were Democrats to cast their votes for him, and to soften the blow somewhat, I told him I thought the rail fence around his picture looked real pretty. Because of the ridicule which overwhelmed me I remember another circumstance. I confided to an older sister that I had written to Mr. Lincoln and she questioned whether I had addressed him properly. I said *I knew I had* and rewrote the address, 'Honorable Abraham Lincoln, Esquire,'—but my mother comforted me by saying in the midst of the laughter that the postmaster would be in no doubt for whom the letter was intended, and this is the reply I received in a few days, a kindly, simple letter from a great-hearted man to a child:

" 'SPRINGFIELD, ILLINOIS, October 19, 1860.

" '*Miss Grace Bedell:*

" 'MY DEAR LITTLE MISS:

" 'Your very agreeable letter of the 15th is received.
I regret the necessity of saying I have no daughter. I
have three sons—one seventeen, one nine, and one seven
years of age. They, with their mother, constitute my
whole family. As to the whiskers, having never worn
any, do you not think people would call it a piece of silly
affectation if I were to begin it now?

" 'Your very sincere well-wisher,

" 'A. LINCOLN.'

"When he made the journey to Washington before
the inauguration he recalled the circumstance when
the train stopped at our town (Westfield, New York)
and called for his little correspondent, giving her name
and the purport of her letter to himself. I was helped
forward and Mr. Lincoln stepped to the platform beside the track, shook my hand and kissed me, saying,
'You see, I let these whiskers grow for you, Grace.' I
was so overcome with confusion that I remember little
else excepting the twinkle which came into his sad eyes
as he held my hand, and the cheers of the assembled
crowd."

"Very truly,

(Signed) "Mrs. Grace Bedell Billings."

It is remarkable that a child should write such a letter to such a man. It is even more remarkable that such
a man should reply to such a letter from a child; that
he should so promptly carry out the suggestion which
her letter contained; and that he should so kindly remember and so cordially greet his "little correspond-

ent" when on his way to assume his grave duties as President of the United States. No action of Lincoln's life ever revealed more completely the greatness of his simplicity than the courtesy shown to his little friend, Grace Bedell.

It is the opinion of Lord Charnwood, to whom is credited "the first considered attempt by an Englishman to give a picture of Lincoln," that few men can be compared with Lincoln in his ability to reduce thought to the simplest and plainest terms possible. All his leading American biographers emphasize this same remarkable power which was shown in his treatment of all the questions with which he had to deal. Lincoln's thinking was always characterized by simplicity. "Given his clear perception of the thing he wanted to do," says Helen Nicolay in *Personal Traits of Abraham Lincoln,* "his direct, simple processes of reasoning would show him a way to do it." Abundant evidence of this can be found in his arguments as a lawyer in presenting a case to the judge or jury, in his discussion of political issues in the various campaigns in which he had a prominent part, in his debates with Douglas, in his messages to Congress, and in other great state papers.

Simplicity of thought always finds expression in language of simplicity. In the use of such language, Lincoln was a master. He never used words of great length whose meaning was not plain to the common people. "Billy, don't shoot too high," he once warned his young law partner, Herndon, who had a tendency to indulge in language of a pretentious nature—"aim lower and the common people will understand you. They are the ones you want to reach—at least they are the ones you ought to reach. The educated and refined people will understand you anyway. If you aim too high, your ideas will go over the heads of the masses, and only hit those who need no hitting."

This advice Lincoln, himself, always followed. His greatest thoughts on the most profound questions were clothed in the simplest language, made up in a large measure of words of one syllable, as the following quotations, selected from a variety of sources, conclusively prove:

"As a nation of freemen we must live through all time or die by suicide."—*Address on the Perpetuation of Our Political Institutions.*

"Stand with anybody that stands right. Stand with him while he is right, and part with him when he goes wrong."—*Speech on the Missouri Compromise.*

"But we must not promise what we ought not, lest we be called on to perform what we cannot."

"Those who deny freedom to others, deserve it not for themselves; and, under the rule of a just God, cannot long retain it."—*Speech delivered at Bloomington, Illinois, May 29, 1856, commonly known as "The Lost Speech."*

"Let us have faith that right makes might; and in that faith let us to the end dare to do our duty as we understand it."—*Cooper Institute Speech.*

"But I have said nothing but what I am willing to live by, and, if it be the pleasure of Almighty God, to die by."—*Address in Independence Hall.*

"Property is the fruit of labor; property is desirable; is a positive good in the world. That some should be rich shows that others may become rich, and hence is just encouragement to industry and enterprise. Let not him who is houseless pull down the house of another, but let him work diligently and build one for himself, thus by example assuring that his own shall be safe from violence when built."—*Remarks to a Committee from the Workingmen's Association of New York.*

"In regard to this great book, I have but to say it is the best gift God has given to man. All the good Savior gave to the world was communicated through this book. But for it we could not know right from wrong."—*Remarks upon the presentation of a Bible by a committee of colored people from Baltimore.*

"Fellow citizens, we cannot escape history. We of this Congress and this administration will be remembered in spite of ourselves. No personal significance or insignificance can spare one or another of us. The fiery trial through which we pass will light us down, in honor or dishonor, to the latest generation. We say we are for the Union. The world will not forget that we say this. We know how to save the Union. The world knows we do know how to save it. We—even we here— hold the power and bear the responsibility. In giving freedom to the slave, we assure freedom to the free— honorable alike in what we give and what we preserve. We shall nobly save or meanly lose the last, best hope of earth. Other means may succeed; this could not fail. The way is plain, peaceful, generous, just— a way which, if followed, the world will forever applaud, and God must forever bless."—*Appeal for Compensated Emancipation, Annual Message to Congress, December 1, 1862.*

"The way for a young man to rise is to improve himself every way he can, never suspecting that anybody wishes to hinder him."—*Letter to William H. Herndon.*

"In law, it is good policy to never plead what you need not, lest you oblige yourself to prove what you cannot."—*Letter to U. F. Linder.*

"Truth to speak, I do not appreciate this matter of rank on paper as you officers do. The world will not forget that you fought the battle of Stone River, and it will never care a fig whether you rank General Grant on paper, or he so ranks you."—*Letter to Major-General Rosecrans.*

The most notable example in all literature of the expression of profound thought and noble, patriotic sentiment in the simplest language, is found in Lincoln's Gettysburg Address. Attention has already been called to the humility which characterizes this Address. In another chapter will be found the history of its preparation and delivery. In this remarkable Address, which is known around the world, and which has been translated into nearly all languages, there are only two hundred and sixty-eight words, including the articles "a" and "the," of which number, one hundred and ninety-six, or seventy-three per cent, are words of one syllable.

And so out of the simplicity in which he was born and reared and from which he never departed, Abraham Lincoln struggled to success and constantly exemplified in thought, word, and deed, the sentiment expressed by Emerson: "Nothing is more simple than greatness; indeed, to be simple is to be great."

CHAPTER VI

LINCOLN'S HUMOR

HUMOR played an important part in the life of Abraham Lincoln. By means of his kindly humor, friends were made and enemies placated. It helped him to endure failure as well as to win success. It kept him from taking himself too seriously and developed in him a generous attitude toward others. It enabled him to see things in their proper relations. It gave him a keen insight into human nature and a sympathetic understanding of the motives which control human actions. It revealed truth and exposed error in such a manner as to influence judges to give opinions and juries to render verdicts in accordance with right and justice, tempered with mercy. It harmonized discordant factions in Cabinet and Congress and thus helped to save the Union.

While little is known of Lincoln's childhood and youth, there is good reason to believe that his humor manifested itself at an early age and that it served to brighten many a dull day in his lonely life as a boy. One instance of his quaintly humorous way of helping a friend in need is related by Herndon and other biographers.

The friend was Kate Roby, a little miss of fifteen.

In the spelling class, the word "defied" was pronounced as it came her turn to spell. "Abe stood on the opposite side of the room," Kate is reported as saying, "and was watching me. I began d-e-f- and then I stopped, hesitating whether to proceed with an 'i' or a 'y.' Looking up I beheld Abe, a grin covering his face, and pointing with his index finger to his eye. I took the hint, spelled the word with an 'i,' and it went through all right."

We are reliably informed that "as a boy Lincoln loved a story for the fun of it," and there is abundant evidence that he cultivated his natural ability to tell stories whenever an opportunity presented itself. The principal story book he had a chance to read was *Aesop's Fables,* which he devoured with intense interest, and which no doubt had a large influence in developing his remarkable power to use an anecdote or an illustration with such telling effect in driving home an argument before a jury or in making plain to his neighbors and friends his views on public questions. His stories were usually taken from the experiences of the pioneer life with which he was familiar. As he quaintly put it, he "did not care to quarry among the ancients for his figures." Whenever he was "reminded" of something that had happened "down in Indiana" or of some experience in "Sangamon County," all who were fortunate enough to be in his company knew that he was preparing the way for a choice story and a good laugh, in which he always heartily joined. In fact, it was his own keen enjoyment of a story which enabled him to tell it with such irresistible effect.

In laughter, he found the tonic which strengthened him to carry his heavy load of responsibility and the relief which made it possible for him to endure the sorrow which was breaking his heart. There were some who were unable to understand how he could ever indulge in levity in the midst of all the sadness caused by the war, and who criticised him unkindly and censured him severely for so doing. To one such, he sadly explained: "If it were not for this occasional vent, I should die."

How many of the stories credited to Lincoln were ever told by him cannot be accurately determined. Certain it is that many of them he never even heard. From the most reliable sources of information we learn that less than a hundred of the so-called "Lincoln stories" are genuine, and Lincoln, himself, is credited with the statement that as near as he could reckon, about one-sixth only of those credited to him were old acquaintances, and that he was only "a retail dealer."

Lincoln's stories were always short. They were always well told. But their unusual effect was due to the fact that they were always apt. They were told not so much for the sake of the story and the laughter it provoked as for the purpose of making plain some important point which he clearly saw and was anxious that others should see. It was his way of realizing the desire of his childhood, which became the passion of his life, to have people comprehend his meaning.

There is a lingering impression, due in part to statements made by a few biographers, but more especially to a tradition which has been handed down through the years, that it was Lincoln's habit, even in ordinary conversation, to indulge in objectionable stories marked by vulgarity in both their content and teaching. There is good reason for the belief that this impression does great injustice to his memory. This belief is based upon the evidence furnished by the most reliable witnesses, who had an intimate acquaintance with his daily life, and who bear testimony to the fact that Lincoln was a remarkably pure-hearted, clean-minded man.

In her *Personal Traits of Abraham Lincoln,* Helen Nicolay refers to the false impression that Lincoln's stories were "coarse," calls attention to one source of the impression, and most conclusively defends him against the charge as follows:

"The life in which he grew up, the life of pioneer times, and of the small village communities which immediately followed it in the Middle West, was poor in culture and refinements of living, but strong in racy human nature. Hence over-fastidious people, who liked 'quarrying among the ancients,' found his stories coarse. Homely would be a truer term, for they were never coarse in spirit, even when most sordid in detail. Ethically they always pointed a clean moral. They were of the soil—strongly of the soil—but never of the charnel-house."

Frank B. Carpenter, the artist who painted the historic picture—The Emancipation Proclamation—literally lived with President Lincoln for six months. In his *Six Months at the White House,* he refers to

the report that Lincoln sometimes indulged in stories
of a questionable nature, and says:

"Mr. Lincoln, I am convinced, has been greatly
wronged in this respect. Every foul-mouthed man in
the country gave currency to the slime and filth of his
own imagination by attributing it to the President. It
is but simple justice to his memory that I should state
that during the entire period of my stay in Washington, after witnessing his intercourse with nearly all
classes of men, embracing governors, senators, members of Congress, officers of the army, and intimate
friends, I can not recollect to have heard him relate a
circumstance to any one of them, which would have
been out of place uttered in a ladies' drawing-room.
And this testimony is not unsupported by that of
others, well entitled to consideration. Dr. Stone, his
family physician, came in one day to see my studies.
Sitting in front of that of the President,—with whom
he did not sympathize politically—he remarked with
much feeling, 'It is the province of a physician to
probe deeply the interior lives of men, and I affirm that
Mr. Lincoln is the purest hearted man with whom I
ever came in contact.' "

It is time that the libel on Lincoln's memory that he
was coarse and vulgar in either thought, word, or
deed, along with those that he was not of legitimate
birth and that he was an infidel and atheist, should receive the denunciation which the truth demands.

A few of the well-authenticated "Lincoln stories"
will serve to illustrate both his humor and the aptness
which always characterized his use of the story.

Two men had a fight. One of them started the row
by using abusive language and by making a bodily attack upon the other. He vigorously defended himself
and completely worsted his assailant. A lawsuit resulted in which the first charged the second with as-
sault and battery. Lincoln defended the man so
charged and in addressing the jury was "reminded"
of the story of a man who, while walking peaceably
along the road with a pitchfork on his shoulder, was
viciously attacked by a ferocious dog belonging to a
neighbor. In using the pitchfork to defend himself,
one of the prongs stuck into the dog and killed him.

"What made you kill my dog?" demanded the angry
owner.

"What made him bite me?" asked the man.

"But why did you not go at him with the other end
of the pitchfork?" inquired the owner.

"Why did he not come at me with his other end?" replied the man.

It is needless to add that the jury greatly enjoyed the
story, heartily appreciated its aptness, readily made
the application, and soon brought in a verdict for the
defendant.

In another case Lincoln defended a client who had
been sued by a neighbor for damages caused to his
growing crops by hogs belonging to the defendant.
There was no question as to the fact that the crops had
been somewhat damaged, but there was conflicting
testimony as to whether or not the plaintiff's fence
was such as to meet the requirements of the law in
being strong enough to keep out stock. In fact, the

whole case hinged on the condition of the fence. Lincoln did not argue the case seriously, as the amount of damages involved was insignificant. The humor of the situation appealed to him and "reminded" him of a story he had heard about "a fence that was so crooked that, when a hog went through an opening in it, invariably it came out on the same side from which it started." He then proceeded to describe in his inimitable manner the bewildered look of the hog after an experience of going through the fence several times and still finding itself on the side from which it first started. The jury joined in the fun, which no doubt influenced them in reaching a verdict.

One of Lincoln's opponents in a political campaign refused to commit himself definitely upon any question. He would either dodge the issue entirely, or else discuss it in such an indefinite or evasive manner as to leave an opening for escape should he be cornered in the future. His actions "reminded" Lincoln of the story of a hunter who boasted of his ability as a marksman. He described how he was able to direct his aim, when in danger of mistaking a calf for a deer, by declaring: "I shot at it so as to hit it if it was a deer, and to miss it if it was a calf."

In one of his political speeches, Lincoln referred to the "Free Soil Party" as representing but one principle with only one plank in its platform. This "reminded" him of the story of a Yankee peddler who sold pantaloons which he highly recommended as being "large enough for any man, and small enough for any boy."

When Simon Cameron, who was Secretary of War in Lincoln's Cabinet for a short time, resigned, some officious friends called on the President to express their gratification at the resignation and to suggest that, in their opinion, the best interests of the country required a complete change in the Cabinet. This suggestion at once "reminded" Lincoln of "Joe Wilson," who had a little log cabin near where he lived in the early days. Being fond of chickens and eggs, "Joe" fitted up a poultry shed and proceeded to raise a fine lot of choice fowls. Being annoyed by repeated visits of skunks, which killed a number of his chickens, he loaded his old musket one night and fired into a group of the pestiferous little animals, only one of which was killed. When asked why he didn't kill the rest, "Joe" replied: "Blast it! Why, it was eleven weeks before I got over killin' one."

One would be over-fastidious indeed to find anything coarse or vulgar in this story which furnished a more complete answer to the foolish suggestion that the entire Cabinet should be changed, than any formal argument which could have been made.

Lincoln was constantly subjected to the most severe and unreasonable criticism. It was his rule to pay no attention to such criticism, however unjust it might be. When he was certain that he was right, the abuse heaped upon him did not disturb him. On one occasion a friend called to express his righteous indignation at what seemed to him an unusually unfair attack from men who were quite prominent in public affairs. "It is not worth fretting about," quietly replied Lincoln, who was "reminded" of an acquaintance who had a young son with an inquiring type of mind. A microscope was given to the boy to help him in his investigations. The lad examined everything within reach, including some cheese which he advised his father not to eat, as it was full of "wigglers." "Let 'em wiggle," was the reply of the father, as he took a larger bite of the cheese than usual, "I can stand it if they can."

All kinds of people volunteered to advise Lincoln as to the conduct of the war. At one time when Washington was threatened by the Confederate forces, a delegation called to suggest that a fleet of war vessels be sent at once to Charleston, Mobile, Savannah, and other cities "to draw off" the army which endangered the safety of the national capital. The suggestion "reminded" Lincoln of a girl in New Salem who was greatly troubled with "singing in her head." Different physicians were consulted but no relief secured. Finally "a common sense sort of man" advised that "a plaster of Psalm tunes" be applied to her feet "to draw the singing down."

When a telegram was received stating that firing was heard in the direction of Knoxville, Lincoln remarked that he was "glad of it." Surprise was expressed that he should be "glad" when Burnside's army might be in danger. He replied that it "reminded" him of "Mistress Sallie Ward," a one-time neighbor, with a large family. Whenever one of her numerous progeny was heard crying in some out-of-the-way place, she would exclaim with apparent satisfaction—"There's one of my family that isn't dead yet."

An old-time friend from New Salem is reported to have related how Lincoln illustrated his doubts as to who was the loser when a tariff was levied on imports, by telling the story of a man who entered a grocery and ordered a nickel's worth of ginger snaps. As he was about to take them, he changed his mind and ordered a glass of cider instead. After drinking the cider, he started to leave, when the following dialogue took place.

"Say, Bill, ain't you goin' to pay me for the cider?"

The customer replied, "Didn't I give you the ginger snaps for it?"

"Well then, pay me for the ginger snaps."

"But, I never ate your ginger snaps," was the answer.

The puzzled groceryman had to admit that both replies were true, but at the same time he knew that he had lost something in the deal. "So it is with the tariff," Lincoln is reported to have said, "somebody loses, but I do not know as yet just who it is."

Among the many perplexing questions which claimed attention during the Civil War was the one relating to San Domingo. In his Message of December 6, 1864, President Lincoln called attention to the fact that "Civil war continues in the Spanish part of San Domingo, apparently without prospect of an early close."

Since the slavery question was involved in the war on the island as well as in our own war, there was danger that serious complications might arise with Spain, which showed a tendency to be more friendly to the North as the war with the South progressed. How to encourage this tendency and at the same time not to offend the abolitionists, who sympathized with the negroes of San Domingo in their struggle for freedom, was a question which caused a great deal of anxiety to Secretary Seward. When he brought the matter before the Cabinet for consideration, the question "reminded" Lincoln of a negro preacher who earnestly reproved one of his members for some of his sins.

"Dar am," said the preacher, "only two roads befo' you. Be careful which one of dem you take. Narrow am de way dat leads straight to destruction; but broad am de road dat leads direct to damnation."

The erring brother opened wide his big eyes and exclaimed—"Parson, you take whichever road you likes best. Dis here darky am gwine to take to de woods!"

The President proceeded to make a fitting application of the story by stating to his Cabinet that he was not willing to assume any new trouble or responsibility at the time, and that he would avoid going to the one place with Spain or to the other with the negroes, by maintaining an honest and strict neutrality.

Story telling, however, was not by any means, the only avenue through which Lincoln's rare humor found expression. His way of putting things in conversation, correspondence, and public address, was often so quaint and droll as to be exceedingly amusing. Many of his letters contain touches of delightful humor.

No one else could have thought of writing such a letter as the following to ask for the renewal of a railroad pass:

"SPRINGFIELD, ILL., FEB. 13, 1856.

"R. P. Morgan, Esq.
"DEAR SIR: Says Tom to John: 'Here's your old rotten wheelbarrow. I've broke it, usin' on it. I wish you would mend it, 'case I shall want to borrow it this arter-noon.'

"Acting on this as a precedent, I say, 'Here's your old chalked hat.' I wish you would take it and send me a new one, 'case I shall want to use it the first of March.

"Yours truly,
"A. LINCOLN."

Having been requested by a New York firm to furnish them with information relative to the financial standing of one of his neighbors, he replied:

"Yours of the 10th received. First of all, he has a wife and baby; together they ought to be worth $500,000 to any man. Secondly, he has an office in which there is a table worth $1.50 and three chairs worth, say $1.00. Last of all, there is in one corner a large rat hole, which will bear looking into.

"Respectfully,
"A. LINCOLN."

While in Congress Lincoln wrote to Herndon, his law partner, calling attention to the losses sustained by the Whigs in his district and urging a more effective organization. Among other things he suggested:

"You young men get together and form a 'Rough and Ready Club,' and have regular meetings and speeches.

Take in everybody you can get. Harrison Grimsley,
L. A. Enos, Lee Kimball, and C. W. Matheney will do to
begin the thing; but as you go along gather up all the
shrewd, wild boys about town, whether just of age or a
little under age,—Chris Logan, Reddick Ridgely, Lewis
Zwizler, and hundreds such. Let every one play the
part he can play best,—some speak, some sing, and all
'holler.' Your meetings will be of evenings; the older
men, and the women, will go to hear you; so that it will
not only contribute to the election of 'Old Zach,' but will
be an interesting pastime, and improving to the intellectual faculties of all engaged. Don't fail to do this."

This furnishes a fine illustration of Lincoln's intimate knowledge of the political situation at home as
well as of his political shrewdness, organizing ability,
and humor, which always kept him human.

In his earlier speeches he sometimes indulged in a
species of rollicking humor which was in keeping with
the times and most effective in securing the desired results. The following incidents will serve as illustra-
tions:

George Forquer, a prominent lawyer, had been a
Whig, and was accused with having forsaken that
party for the appointment of Register of the Land
Office. His new house was protected with a lightning
rod, then a new device, and the first one seen by Lincoln. He attended a meeting addressed by Lincoln
in one of his campaigns for election to the legislature,
and asked to be heard. The crowd, anxious for some
fun, signified their wish that the request be granted.
Forquer assumed a haughty attitude and introduced
his insulting remarks with the statement that "this

young man would have to be taken down." His inso-
lent manner thoroughly roused Lincoln. He replied
to the attack with a vigor which surprised all who
heard him, and then turned his attention to Forquer,
personally:

> "This anomalous Forquer, if he has taken me *down*,
> as he calls it, I reckon you know it, and if he is satis-
> fied, I am. He seems to be thoroughly up to political
> tricks—something I am not familiar with, and I never
> intend to be. If I can't get office honestly, I am content
> to live as I am, and I hope I never may be so thoroughly
> steeped in political trickery as to change my political
> coat for a big office, and then feel so guilty about it as
> to run up a lightning rod to protect my house from the
> vengeance of an offended God."

In another of Lincoln's campaigns, "Dick" Taylor
was one of the Democratic "orators" who opposed him.
Taylor was a professional politician who, along with
his brother, had held office the greater part of his life.
In one of his speeches he made an appeal to the prej-
udices of the crowd by ridiculing the Whigs, speaking of them as "bankers and toadies to the English"—
representatives of aristocracy. He lauded his own
party as the friend of the poor man, and characterized
by simplicity and honest purposes. Taylor, himself,
was a fop who always wore a ruffled shirt, blue coat,
and brass buttons, oiled his hair with great care, and
carried a gold-headed cane. As he closed his demagog-
ic appeal, Lincoln caught hold of his vest, suddenly
jerked it open, and thus exposed to the view of the
jeering crowd the ruffled shirt, the ponderous watch
chain and other ornaments which had been carefully,

concealed for the occasion. With this striking object lesson to attract the attention of his hearers, Lincoln proceeded to address them:

"And here's Dick Taylor charging us with aristocracy and gilt manners, and claiming to be an exponent of the farmers and cattle-raisers; and while he's doing this, he stands in a hundred-dollar suit of clothes, in a dancing-master's pomp and parade, with a ruffled shirt just such as his master, General Jackson, wears, and a gold log-chain around his neck to keep his watch from being stole by some of us, and with a big gold-headed cane. And while he was raised in this style, I was a-steering a flatboat down the river for eight dollars a month; with a torn shirt, one pair of buckskin breeches, and a *warmus* as my only suit. The Bible says, 'By their fruits ye shall know them'; now I have got on my best to-day, and Taylor has got on his shabbiest. You can judge which one of us is the aristocrat by our appearance."

In the campaign of 1848, the friends of Lewis Cass attempted to make political capital out of his rather obscure service on the frontier in the War of 1812. Their actions amused Lincoln, who made a speech in Congress in which he cleverly ridiculed their efforts by humorously referring to his own military experience in the Black Hawk War:

"Did you know," said he in addressing the Speaker, "I am a military hero? Yes, sir; in the days of the Black Hawk War I fought, bled, and came away. Speaking of General Cass's career reminds me of my own. I was not at Stillman's defeat, but I was about as near it as Cass was to Hull's surrender; and, like him, I saw the place very soon afterward. It is quite certain I did

LINCOLN STATUE

This statue of Lincoln, at Hodgenville, Kentucky, is the work of the
well-known sculptor Adolph Weinman.

LINCOLN MEMORIAL AT WASHINGTON

In the portico is a statue of Lincoln, seated, the work of the noted sculptor, Daniel Chester French.

not break my sword, for I had none to break; but I bent
a musket pretty badly on one occasion. If Cass broke
his sword, the idea is he broke it in desperation; I
bent the musket by accident. If General Cass went in
advance of me in picking huckleberries, I guess I surpassed him in charges upon the wild onions. If he saw
any live, fighting Indians, it was more than I did; but I
had a good many bloody struggles with the mosquitoes,
and, although I never fainted from the loss of blood, I
can truly say I was often very hungry."

In commenting upon Lincoln's campaign speeches,
the Nicolay and Hay *Life* observes that "he never
took his campaigning seriously." This was no doubt
true in his early campaigns in which relatively unim-
portant subjects were under discussion. But it is
important to note that in his later campaigns when the
issues involved grave moral and political questions,
such as slavery and the preservation of the Union, he
was always intensely in earnest and reverently serious.

One will look in vain in the Cooper Institute Speech
for any trace of the humor for which Lincoln's earlier
speeches were noted. Different persons who heard
the Lincoln-Douglas Debates have left on record their
impression of the seriousness which characterized Lincoln in that great contest. When he was urged by his
friends to put more humor into the discussion and was
told that the people would be disappointed if he did
not, he replied that he could not do so, because of the
seriousness of the question under consideration. In
fact, Lincoln's humor, which so often manifested itself in such an inimitable manner, never intruded
where seriousness had a right to be.

Lincoln's keenest humor is found in the observations which often flashed from his alert mind in the form of pertinent remarks which so completely answered a criticism or met a condition under consideration as to leave nothing to be said.

On one occasion a prominent senator called on the President to urge the removal of General Grant. One of his remarks "reminded" Lincoln of a story, the mere mention of which threw the Senator into a passion to which he gave vent by saying:

"It is with you, sir, all story, story! You are the father of every military blunder that has been made during the war. You are on your road to hell, sir, with this government, by your obstinacy; and you are not a mile off at this minute." To this outburst, Lincoln quietly replied: "Senator, that is just about the distance from here to the Capitol, is it not?"

It is related that the Senator grabbed up his hat and cane and indignantly left the White House, but soon came to his senses as he realized the humor of the situation, and returned in a very different frame of mind.

At the opening of the Civil War, the state of Maryland protested against sending troops across her territory on their way to Washington. A delegation composed of representatives of one of the religious bodies of Baltimore, with a clergyman as their spokesman, called on President Lincoln to join in the protest and even to propose that he should "recognize the independence of the Southern States." Lincoln's patience was sorely taxed, but, as usual, he kept his temper.

His reply, which contained a vein of humor, left no doubt as to his intentions. He said in part:

"Your citizens attack troops sent to the defense of the Government, and the lives and property in Washington, and yet you would have me break my oath and surrender the Government without a blow. There is no Washington in that—no Jackson in that—there is no manhood or honor in that. I have no desire to invade the South; but I must have troops to defend this capital. Geographically it lies surrounded by the soil of Maryland; and mathematically the necessity exists that they should come over her territory. Our men are not moles, and can't dig under the earth; they are not birds, and can't fly through the air. There is no way but to march across and that they must do. But in doing this, there is no need of collision. Keep your rowdies in Baltimore, and there will be no bloodshed. Go home and tell your people that if they will not attack us, we will not attack them, but if they do attack us, we will return it, and that severely."

One day, a woman of haughty mien called upon President Lincoln and insolently demanded that her son be given a commission as colonel. She insisted that he had a right to such recognition because her grandfather had fought at Lexington, her uncle had shown unusual bravery at Bladensburg, her father had been in the battle of New Orleans, and her husband had been killed at Monterey. After listening patiently to this dramatic recital of family history, he calmly and courteously replied that he thought her family had done enough for the country and that some one else should be given a chance.

At another time a self-appointed delegation called

at the White House to criticise the Administration for what they deemed its mistakes of omission and commission. As usual Lincoln listened patiently and then replied with the use of an illustration which, while quaintly humorous in the picture presented, completely answered their complaints:

"Gentlemen," said he, "suppose all the property you were worth was in gold, and you had put it in the hands of Blondin (famous tight-rope performer of that time) to carry across the Niagara River on a rope, would you shake the cable, or keep shouting out to him, 'Blondin, stand up a little straighter—Blondin, stoop a little more, go a little faster—lean a little more to the North,—lean a little more to the South? No, you would hold your breath as well as your tongue, and keep your hands off until he was safe over. The Government are carrying an immense weight. Untold treasures are in their hands. They are doing the very best they can. Don't badger them. Keep silence, and we'll get you safe across."

One of Lincoln's intimate friends wanted to visit a brother-in-law, a good Union man, who lived in Virginia. He called on General Halleck for a pass to go outside the lines for that purpose and was refused. He appealed to Secretary of War Stanton with the same result. He related his experience to President Lincoln, who smilingly replied: "I can do nothing for you; for you must know that I have very little influence with this administration."

Lincoln's patience was such as to lead him to listen with courtesy to all sorts of recommendations and schemes for the supposed betterment of humanity.

After an attentive hearing to a tedious presentation of a visionary plan for an "ideal community," he was asked for an expression of his opinion, and replied: "For those who like that sort of thing that is the sort of thing they like."

It is not difficult to imagine the surprise which must have come to the aristocratic senator Charles Sumner who, when in search of President Lincoln, was told that he was downstairs, where he found him polishing his boots. But it is difficult to realize the shock which his senatorial dignity must have suffered, when in response to his protest, "Why, Mr. President, do you black your own boots?" he received the laughing reply, "Whose boots did you think I was blacking?"

All Presidents have been subjected to great annoyance in making appointments—none more so than Lincoln. It is difficult to realize in these days, when civil service laws have greatly reduced the number of political appointments, what he had to endure from the horde of office seekers seeking preferment from him.

Early in his administration when he was doing all in his power to avert the threatened Civil War, and was constantly besieged by applicants for office, he remarked that the situation was not unlike that of a man who was busy renting rooms at one end of his house, while the other was in flames.

On another occasion, after the war had begun, when he appeared much depressed, an anxious friend asked whether the loss of another battle was the cause. "No," replied Lincoln, "it's the post office at—," an insignificant hamlet in a western state.

In such perplexities, Lincoln's humor usually came to the rescue. A fine illustration of this is found in his reply to a delegation of distinguished men who called to urge the appointment of a friend for Commissioner to the Sandwich Islands. With eloquent earnestness they argued that the appointment they sought would be of great value not only to the United States, because of the character and ability of their candidate, but also to the man, himself, whose declining health would be greatly benefited by the climate of the Islands. "I am very sorry to say," replied Lincoln, after listening good-humoredly to their presentation, "that there are eight other candidates for the place, all sicker than your man."

The "red tape" which has always characterized military procedure was a constant source of disturbance to Lincoln, who had little patience or sympathy with the unnecessary delay often caused by official formality. Evidence of this, together with another illustration of his unfailing humor, is found in his letter to Secretary of War Stanton:

"I personally wish Jacob Freeze of New Jersey to be appointed Colonel for a colored regiment, and this regardless of whether he can tell the exact shade of Julius Caesar's hair."

Notwithstanding the fact that he was a member of the Cabinet, Secretary of the Treasury Chase was unsparing in his criticism of President Lincoln. At different times, in a fit of indignation because he could not have his own way, or because of some imaginary slight, he resigned. Finally his resignation was accepted, June 30, 1864, and he retired from the Cabinet. He did not hesitate to encourage Lincoln's outspoken enemies in their attempt to defeat him for renomination, and gave his approval to the movement in behalf of his own candidacy.

A few months after his retirement from the Cabinet, Chief-Justice Taney of the United States Supreme Court died. The friends of Chase at once began to insist that he should be appointed to fill the vacancy. Letters of recommendation poured in from all sections of the country. While it is probable that Lincoln intended from the first to appoint him, he gave no intimation of his intentions until the appointment was made, remarking to his secretary,—"I shall be very 'shut pan' about this matter." One day his attention was called to a letter from Chase himself. "What is it about?" inquired the President. "Simply a kind and friendly letter," answered the secretary. Without reading it, and with exquisite humor, reinforced with a shrewd smile, Lincoln replied: "File it with his other recommendations."

The "radical element" of Lincoln's day, so far as his own party was concerned, consisted largely of the men with extreme antislavery sentiments, who were determined, if possible, to defeat his renomination. Finding that this would be impossible, a number of "informal consultations" were held, with the result that a "Mass Convention of the People" was called to meet in Cleveland, Ohio, the week before the Baltimore Convention at which Lincoln was renominated. This "Mass Convention," which was not largely attended, denounced the administration of Lincoln, and nominated John C. Fremont, who later withdrew his name from the list of candidates.

While Lincoln's friends were excited and indignant at the whole proceeding, he was greatly amused. When he was informed that the attendance at the Convention, instead of numbering thousands as had been predicted, never included more than four hundred men, his sense of humor at once suggested that the second verse of the twenty-second chapter of First Samuel well described the situation. Acting upon the suggestion, he picked up his Bible, which lay on his desk, and to the delight of all present, read:

"And every one that was in distress, and every one that was in debt, and every one that was discontented, gathered themselves unto him; and he became a captain over them: and there were with him about four hundred men."

On February 3, 1865, the historic Hampton Roads Conference was held on board the *River Queen*, near Fort Monroe, where President Lincoln and Secretary Seward met Messrs. Stephens, Hunter, and Campbell, who were delegated to represent the Southern Confederacy as "Peace Commissioners." At this conference, as at all other places and times, President Lincoln was unalterable in his insistence that no proposition looking to an armistice could be entertained until it was settled that the Union was to be restored, and that even if the Confederate States would consider a return to the Union, he could not enter into any agreement of any kind with parties who were in arms

against the government.   In reply to the suggestion
of one of the "Peace Commissioners" that Charles I
of England had treated with the people who were in
arms against him, Lincoln replied:

"I do not pretend to be posted in history.   On all
such matters I will turn you over to Seward.   All I
distinctly recollect about Charles I is that he lost his
head."

No finer humor can be found than that which flowed
so freely from the keen brain and kind heart of Abraham Lincoln.   It furnishes a pleasant and profitable
study which it is well to make in order that justice
may be done to his memory.   Too often, however, the
impression has been left by those who have written or
spoken of Lincoln's life that he was "a sort of end-man
with an itinerant minstrel show," as he travelled the
historic Eighth Judicial District of Illinois.

One of Lincoln's most intimate friends, who travelled with him on that district, has described how "he
would frequently lapse into reverie and remain lost in
thought" long after his companions had gone to bed;
and how sometimes in the early morning he would be
found "sitting before the fire, his mind apparently
concentrated on some subject and with the saddest expression. . . . . ever seen in a human being's eyes."

"No one knows," writes this friend, "with what
thoughts Lincoln was struggling in those hours, but
this side of his character has almost disappeared under
the mass of silly stories which are coupled with his
name.   One would think, to read some of the biogra-
phies, that he never had a serious moment, and that

most of his life on the circuit was spent in retailing
dubious stories to gaping circles of country-folk at
wayside taverns."

No one will ever know "with what thoughts Lincoln was struggling in those hours." It is known, however, that when the time came to free the slaves and
save the Union, he was prepared to lead the way because he had thought his way through the problems of
the relation of slavery to the Union as no one else had
done. It was no accident, as some would have us believe, that he was called to leadership in the nation's
greatest crisis.

Perhaps he may have had, in those long hours of
solemn reverie and serious thought, a vision of the
terrible responsibility which he was later on to be
called to assume, together with the heart-breaking
sorrow which was to be his. But when the responsibility and sorrow came, it was his sense of humor
that helped him to bear them. For it will be recalled
that he, himself, has told us that but for that "occasional vent" he would have died.

CHAPTER VII

LINCOLN'S MAGNANIMITY

AS humility was the foundation upon which the sterling character of Abraham Lincoln was built, so magnanimity was the crowning virtue of his remarkable life. Like all words of large meaning, magnanimity is difficult to define. It includes greatness of mind and exaltation of soul. It enables its possessor to rise above all that is little and low. It will not stoop to revenge. It despises injustice, hates wrong, and disdains meanness. It is calmly courageous in the midst of danger and difficulty. It is kind under all circumstances and remains patient even in the presence of insult and injury. It exercises self-control when provoked, and is willing to make personal sacrifice to attain a noble purpose. All these characteristics which are included in magnanimity, Lincoln exemplified to an unusual degree.

His kindness is proverbial. The sight of suffering either in human beings or in animals aroused his keen sense of sympathy and led him to do all in his power to relieve it. When fully grown, he did not think it unmanly to go out of his way to replace a fluttering bird in the nest from which it had fallen. When serving as a member of the legislature of his state, on

one of his homeward journeys, he did not deem it un-
dignified to retrace his steps and engage in the menial
service of releasing an unfortunate pig that had been
caught under the fence, remarking that he felt much
better after relieving its distress.

On the frontier where Lincoln grew up, almost
every youth was an excellent marksman. Hunting
was greatly enjoyed as a sport and was one of the
chief means of food supply, game of all kinds being
plentiful. Because of his unusual kindness of heart,
Lincoln differed in this particular from all the boys
around him. Hunting was the one sport in which he
never took any pleasure. He could not bear the
thought of killing or inflicting pain.

It is related that when Lincoln was once asked what
he remembered about the war of 1812 with England,
he replied: "Only this: I had been fishing one day
and had caught a little fish, which I was taking home.
I met a soldier in the road, and having always been
told at home that we must be good to soldiers, I gave
him my fish."

In this simple childish act may be found a prophecy
of the great-hearted President's kindness to the soldiers of the Civil War, with whose hardships and trials
he sympathized so keenly. This kindness often led him
to interfere to save the life of some soldier boy who
was under sentence of death by military authority
because of violation of the military code. Numerous
instances of such interference are recorded. One relates to a New England boy who volunteered to stand
guard for a sick comrade. Having gone without sleep

for forty-eight hours, he was so overcome with weariness that he fell asleep at his post, which was near the enemy. He was tried, found guilty, and sentenced to be shot. President Lincoln went to the tent where he was kept under guard, awaiting his execution the following day. In the most kindly manner, he talked with the boy about his early life, and his home and mother. The lad quietly responded by taking his mother's picture from his pocket and showing it to the President, who was deeply moved. Laying his hand gently on the prisoner's shoulder, he said: "My boy, you are not going to be shot to-morrow. I believe you when you tell me you could not keep awake. I am going to trust you, and send you back to your regiment. Now, I want to know what you intend to pay for all this?"

Thinking only of pay in money, all that the poor boy could reply was that he did not know. He sadly recalled the poverty of his people, his own small pay, and an insignificant sum in the savings bank. A ray of hope came with the thought of the possibility of borrowing something by mortgaging the little home farm and of securing help from his comrades in the army. From all these sources, he told the President that it might be possible to raise five or six hundred dollars, and then pathetically asked whether that would be enough. It is not difficult to imagine the relief which came to the grief-stricken soldier in the reply of the President that he was the only man in the world who could pay the bill by so faithfully and loyally serving his country as a soldier that when death came, he could truthfully say that he had kept his promise to the President to do his duty. With a joyful heart he returned to his regiment where, a few months later, he was killed in battle. The promise had been kept. The duty had been performed. The debt had been paid.

While the truthfulness of this incident has been questioned, it so faithfully portrays the characteristic magnanimity of Lincoln that it is believed to be worthy of repetition.

The war department repeatedly protested against the President's leniency in dealing with soldiers who were under sentence from a court-martial, declaring that the discipline of the army was being undermined and its efficiency destroyed by the numerous pardons granted. As a rule Lincoln was unmoved by such protests, sometimes saying in reply that he did not think shooting a soldier would do him any good, anyhow. "Military cowardice" was the technical phrase often used in the charges preferred against soldiers whose cases were referred to the President. In filing them for future consideration, he labeled them "Leg Cases." He fully sympathized with a soldier boy who became frightened in battle and not infrequently was reminded of the Irishman who declared that while he had a heart as brave as ever beat in a human bosom, yet in the presence of danger, his cowardly legs would often run away with him. That Lincoln, himself, realized that the pardons granted by him were quite numerous is indicated in his quaint remarks to Marshal Lamon, who had called to get one signed. "Lamon," said he, "have you ever heard how the Patagonians eat oysters? They open them and throw the shells out of the window until the pile gets higher than the house, and then they move. I feel to-day like commencing a new pile of pardons, and I may just as well sign it just here."

Lincoln's kindness of heart led him to be generous in his treatment of foes as well as of friends. On the last day he lived on earth he talked with his Cabinet about the magnanimous plans for reconstruction which he had in mind and which he hoped would help to restore good will between the North and the South. Referring to the men who had been responsible for bringing on the war, he said no one need expect that he "could take any part in hanging or killing these men, even the worst of them." It is significant that his last official act was writing "Let it be done" on the petition of a Confederate prisoner who wanted to swear allegiance to the Union.

Had he lived, there can be no doubt that he would have done all in his power "to bind up the nation's wounds," literally "with malice toward none; with charity for all."

"I am a patient man, always willing to forgive on the Christian terms of repentance, and also to give ample time for repentance," President Lincoln once wrote to a man in Louisiana who had complained of the methods which were being used to save the government. That he was "a patient man" was constantly exemplified in his life. Certainly no human being ever had his patience more severely tested.

"His kindness and patience in dealing with the generals who did not succeed is the wonder of all who study the history of the Civil War," is the expressed conviction of one of his most competent biographers. A most striking illustration of this is found in the kindness and patience shown to General George B. McClellan in return for the most unkind and humiliating treatment to which President Lincoln was subjected during the trying days of the war. General McClellan had been called to Washington after the defeat at Bull Run and given command of the rapidly growing army. Although successful as an organizer, he failed as a commander. This failure was due in part to his insufferable conceit, which led him to imagine that he, and he alone, had "become the power of the land," to quote his own words. All others, including General Scott, with whom he quarreled, and the President, himself, were beneath his notice and unworthy of his consideration. An example of the contempt with which he treated President Lincoln, who was doing all in his power to help him to succeed, is given by Nicolay and Hay:

"The friendly visits of the President to army headquarters were continued almost every night until the 13th of November, when an incident occurred which virtually put an end to them. On that evening Mr. Lincoln walked across the street as usual, accompanied by one of his household, to the residence of the Secretary of State, and after a short visit there both of them went to General McClellan's house on H Street. They were there told that the General had

ABRAHAM LINCOLN
From a statue by V. Vanucci

LINCOLN FAMILY AT THE WHITE HOUSE

Between the President and Mrs. Lincoln is Robert, the eldest son. The youngest son, Thomas ("Tad"), stands beside Lincoln.

gone to the wedding of an officer and would soon return. They waited nearly an hour in the drawing room, when McClellan returned and, without paying any special attention to the orderly who told him the President was waiting to see him, went upstairs. The President, thinking his name had not been announced, again sent a servant to his room and received the answer that he had gone to bed. Mr. Lincoln attached no special importance to this incident, and, so far as we know, never asked for an explanation nor received one. But it was not unnatural for him to infer that his frequent visits had become irksome to the General. There was no cessation of their friendly relations, though after this most of their conferences were held at the Executive Mansion."

General Fremont, who had been a candidate for President in 1856, was given an important command at Saint Louis. Extremely radical in his opinions, erratic in judgment, rash in action, and unwilling to take advice, he was a constant source of embarrassment to the Administration, until, being unwilling to serve in a position to which he had been appointed, he was relieved at his own request. But through all the trying experiences resulting from the actions of McClellan, Fremont, and other generals, President Lincoln's kindness was constantly shown. His patience never failed.

There were times when the failure of the military authorities to follow up success in battle and thereby to secure the full fruits of victory, brought bitter disappointment to Lincoln and most severely tested his patience. It was in the midst of the disappointment resulting from such failure after the battle of Gettysburg, that he wrote to General Meade, who had been urged to pursue Lee's Army, and who felt so keenly the expressed dissatisfaction with his failure to do so, that he asked to be relieved of the command of the army. In the historic letter published in the Nicolay and Hay *Life,* Lincoln said:

"I have just seen your dispatch to General Halleck asking to be relieved of your command because of a supposed censure of mine. I am very, very grateful to you for the magnificent success you gave the cause of the country at Gettysburg; and I am sorry now to be the author of the slightest pain to you. But I was in such deep distress myself that I could not restrain some expression of it. I have been oppressed nearly ever since the battles at Gettysburg by what appeared to be evidences that yourself and General Couch and General Smith were not seeking a collision with the enemy, but were trying to get him across the river without another battle. What these evidences were, if you please, I hope to tell you at some time when we shall both feel better. The case, summarily stated, is this: You fought and beat the enemy at Gettysburg; and, of course, to say the least, his loss was as great as yours. He retreated, and you did not, as it seemed to me, pressingly pursue him; but a flood in the river detained him till, by slow degrees, you were again upon him. You had at least twenty thousand veteran troops directly with you, and as many more raw ones within supporting distance, all in addition to those who fought with you at Gettysburg; while it was not possible that he had received a single recruit; and yet you stood and let the flood run down, bridges be built, and the enemy move away at his leisure without attacking him. And Couch and Smith—the latter left Carlisle in time, upon all ordinary calculation, to have aided you in the last battle at Gettysburg, but he did not arrive. At the end of more than ten days, I believe, twelve, under constant urging, he reached Hagerstown from Carlisle, which is not an inch over fifty-five miles, if so much, and Couch's movement was very little different.

"Again, my dear General, I do not believe you appreciate the magnitude of the misfortune involved in Lee's escape. He was within your easy grasp, and to have closed upon him, would, in connection with our other late successes, have ended the war. As it is, the war will be prolonged indefinitely. If you could not safely attack Lee last Monday, how can you possibly do so south of the river, when you can take with you very few more than two-thirds of the force you then had in hand? It would be unreasonable to expect, and I do not expect (that) you can now effect much. Your golden opportunity is gone, and I am distressed immeasurably because of it.

"I beg you will not consider this a prosecution or persecution of yourself. As you had learned that I was dissatisfied, I have thought it best to kindly tell you why."

That he should have written this letter is not at all surprising. The marvel is that General Meade never received it. Lincoln's magnanimity—his greatness of mind, kindness of heart, and spirit of forgiveness, —quickly overcame his momentary impatience. The unsigned letter was put in his desk and never sent.

The night of November 6, 1860, Lincoln spent in the Springfield telegraph office upon special invitation of the superintendent. There he read the dispatches which announced his election to the Presidency, together with the shower of congratulatory messages which poured in from friends in all sections of the country. There, with a deep consciousness of the mighty task and the heavy responsibility which his election brought, he tells us that he substantially completed the framework of his Cabinet. That this framework was wisely constructed, after events most conclusively proved. As the leading members of his Cabinet, he selected two of his prominent competitors for the nomination to the Presidency, William H. Seward of New York for Secretary of State, and Salmon P. Chase of Ohio for Secretary of the Treasury. Each had served his state with distinction as governor and United States Senator. Both were recognized as men of ability and character, well qualified in all respects to perform the important duties to which they had been called.

It is interesting, even at this day, to conjecture what may have passed through the minds of these men, so widely experienced in the affairs of state, as they met for the first time in Cabinet session under the new President whose experience in public life had been confined to service in his state legislature, and to one term in the Congress of the United States. He had little personal knowledge of them and they, no doubt, "looked upon him as a simple frontier lawyer at most, and a rival to whom chance had transferred the honor they felt to be due to themselves." Under the circumstances, it is not surprising that they considered themselves superior to the President, and were inclined to assume the role of leadership to which his position entitled him.

Secretary Seward was the first to manifest this attitude. During the first month of the new Administration he was busy in the performance of what he, no doubt, deemed his legitimate official duties. He knew, perhaps more than any other man, what had transpired in Washington during the months which had intervened between Lincoln's election and inauguration and was using his knowledge, together with his powers of mediation and conciliation, to direct the affairs of state in the midst of the alarming conditions which existed. But the performance of his legitimate duties did not seem fully to satisfy his ambition, and on April 1, 1860, he presented "Some Thoughts for the President's Consideration" which plainly indicated a doubt in his own mind as to the President's ability either to formulate or to execute a policy to meet the needs of the time, together with his own willingness to direct the affairs of the government.

This remarkable document opened with a specific criticism of the new Administration—"We are at the end of a month's administration, and yet without a policy, either domestic or foreign."

It contained equally specific recommendations for an extensive and radical policy for the conduct of the threatened war and for the guidance of the United States in its relations with foreign nations, even suggesting a war with France and Spain, under certain conditions. Following these surprising recommendations came the astounding suggestions—

"But whatever policy we adopt, there must be an energetic prosecution of it. For this purpose it must be somebody's business to pursue and direct it incessantly.

"Either the President must do it, himself, and be all the while active in it, or

"Devolve it on some member of his Cabinet. Once adopted, debates on it must end, and all agree and abide.

"It is not my especial province.

"But I neither seek to evade nor assume responsibility."

Whatever may have been the feelings of the President when he read "The Thoughts" presented for his consideration by the leading member of his Cabinet, his perfect self-control enabled him at once to send a reply, which revealed no trace of impatience or indignation, and which conclusively settled the question in dispute.

EXECUTIVE MANSION, April 1, 1861.

Hon. W. H. Seward.

MY DEAR SIR: Since parting with you I have been considering your paper dated this day, and entitled "Some Thoughts for the President's Consideration." The first proposition in it is, "First, We are at the end of a month's administration, and yet without a policy, either domestic or foreign."

At the beginning of that month, in the inaugural, I said: "The power confided to me will be used to hold, occupy, and possess the property and places belonging to the government, and to collect the duties and imposts." This had your distinct approval at the time;

and, taken in connection with the order I immediately gave General Scott, directing him to employ every means in his power to strengthen and hold the forts, comprises the exact domestic policy you now urge, with the single exception that it does not propose to abandon Fort Sumter.

Again, I do not perceive how the reenforcement of Fort Sumter would be done on a slavery or party issue, while that of Fort Pickens would be on a more national and patriotic one.

The news received yesterday in regard to St. Domingo certainly brings a new item within the range of our foreign policy; but up to that time we have been preparing circulars and instructions to ministers and the like, all in perfect harmony, without even a suggestion that we had no foreign policy.

Upon your closing propositions—that "whatever policy we adopt, there must be an energetic prosecution of it.

"For this purpose it must be somebody's business to pursue and direct it incessantly.

"Either the President must do it himself, and be all the while active in it, or

"Devolve it on some member of his Cabinet. Once adopted, debates on it must end, and all agree and abide"—I remark that if this must be done, I must do it. When a general line of policy is adopted, I apprehend there is no danger of its being changed without good reason, or continuing to be a subject of unnecessary debate; still, upon points arising in its progress I wish, and suppose I am entitled to have, the advice of all the Cabinet.

Your obedient servant,

A. LINCOLN.

This remarkable letter is additional evidence of Lincoln's forbearance and of his ability to rise above mere personal considerations in his dealings with others. Even more remarkable is the fact that, so far as is known, the knowledge of its contents was confined to the President and Secretary Seward and that neither of them ever alluded to it afterward. The President put the correspondence away in an envelope and it was not made public until several years after his death. Secretary Seward graciously recognized the greatness and magnanimity of his Chief, became his devoted friend, and loyally served at the head of his Cabinet until the end.

The unquestioned ability and integrity of Secretary Chase admirably fitted him to take charge of the nation's finances in the crucial days of the Civil War, when vast sums of money had to be raised to defray the expenses of the government. But unfortunately he possessed other characteristics which made it almost impossible for him to work in harmony with other members of the Cabinet. He was opinionated, petulant, envious, unsparing in his criticisms of his associates, and always ready to encourage such criticism by others. Much of this criticism related to Secretary Seward, against whom a strong feeling of hostility developed in the Senate. This feeling grew to such an extent that, in a caucus to consider the matter, it was voted to demand his dismissal from the Cabinet. While this rash action was later on modified to take the form of a request that President Lincoln should reconstruct his Cabinet, the original purpose to secure the resignation or removal of Secretary Seward remained unchanged. Learning of the action of the caucus, both the Secretary and his son, the Assistant Secretary, offered their resignations to the President, before he had been formally notified of such action by the committee of the Senate appointed for that purpose.

It was in this grave crisis, which was the cause of great anxiety on the part of President Lincoln, and which severely tested his patience and forbearance, that his greatness of soul and keenness of mind once more came to the rescue, and won a victory which conclusively proved that he was indeed a "master of men." His method of procedure in dealing with the warring factions in both his Cabinet and the Senate furnishes an interesting study.

On the day after the Senate had determined to request that the Cabinet be reconstructed, a committee called upon President Lincoln to present the resolutions which had been adopted. In the long conference which followed, the different members of the committee voiced their opposition to Secretary Seward, dwelling especially upon what they considered his failure to give cordial support to the antislavery measures of the Administration, to the success of which Secretary Chase was earnestly devoted. The conference adjourned to meet again in the evening.

A meeting of the Cabinet was immediately called by President Lincoln who, with characteristic frankness, related what had taken place at the conference with the committee from the Senate, quaintly remarking—"While they seemed to believe in my honesty, they also appeared to think that when I had any good purpose or intention Seward contrived to suck it out

of me unperceived." After assuring the members of
the Cabinet that he needed the services of all of them
and that he did not desire the resignation of any of
them he dismissed them with the request that they
meet him again in the evening. When the committee
of the Senate and the members of the Cabinet, with
the exception of Secretary Seward, met the President
in the evening, according to agreement, they were
greatly surprised to find that it was to be a joint meeting with such a free and open discussion as to make it
impossible for any one, either in the Senate or Cabinet, to claim in the future that anything had been concealed or misrepresented. President Lincoln took
charge of the joint meeting, stated the case at issue,
read the resolutions passed by the Senate, and made
some characteristic comments. In the exceptionally
frank discussion which followed, the Cabinet was
rather sharply criticised in general and Secretary
Seward in particular. They in turn defended themselves and their absent associate with vigor and
dignity.

To Secretary Chase, the discussion was exceedingly
humiliating, as he was compelled to listen to criticisms
of Secretary Seward by the members of the committee
of the Senate, which were in substance a repetition of
the expressions which he, himself, had often used in
talking with the members of the committee about his
colleague in the Cabinet. A most embarrassing situation confronted him in the presence of both parties to
the dispute. He could not join the committee of the
Senate in their attack upon the Cabinet and the Ad-

ministration which they represented. His unkind and unjust criticism of both President Lincoln and Secretary Seward, in which he had freely indulged in the presence of the senators, made ineffective any defense which he might offer in behalf of the Cabinet of which he was a member. Late at night, the joint meeting closed "in a milder spirit than it met," to quote a phrase from Secretary Welles. The controversy clearly revealed the weakness of Secretary Chase, resulting from the jealous, envious, and deceitful traits of an otherwise strong character, and the strength of President Lincoln, who never lost his self-control and who constantly manifested that magnanimity and spirit of fairness which enabled him to decide every question upon its merits, without reference to the effect of the decision upon his own personal success or welfare.

Throughout the whole proceeding, President Lincoln had one definite purpose in mind. He wanted to be in a position where he could refuse to accept the resignation of Secretary Seward without forfeiting the support of the senators who were insisting upon his removal from the Cabinet, and who were friendly to Secretary Chase. In fact, he was anxious to retain both. The realization of his purpose was made possible the morning after the joint meeting, when Secretary Chase, with evident reluctance, tendered his resignation, which was accepted with such alacrity and apparent gratification as to be both surprising and disappointing to the Secretary, who had the habit of resigning when matters did not go to his liking. With the resignations of both secretaries in his hands, President Lincoln was in complete control of the situation. In his own inimitable manner, he remarked: "Now I can ride; I have got a pumpkin in each end of my bag." He at once sent the following identical note to Secretary Seward and to Secretary Chase:

"You have respectively tendered me your resignations as Secretary of State and Secretary of the Treasury of the United States. I am apprised of the circumstances which may render this course personally desirable to each of you; but after most anxious consideration my deliberate judgment is that the public interest does not admit of it. I therefore have to request that you will resume the duties of your Departments respectively."

Both acceded to the request of the President. Secretary Seward acted with commendable promptness, replying the next morning: "I have cheerfully resumed the functions of this Department, in obedience to your command." Secretary Chase was not so prompt. He first wrote a brief letter, saying, "My reflections strengthen my conviction that being once honorably out of the Cabinet, no important public interest now requires my return to it. If I yield this judgment, it will be in deference to apprehensions which really seem to me unfounded. I will sleep on it." He could not get over the feeling of wounded pride which resulted from his observation of the gratification with which his resignation had been accepted. He again wrote the President that he did not want him to decline to accept his resignation, but did not at once send the letter. After learning that Secretary Seward had resumed his duties, he finally concluded that he ought "to conform his action to the President's judgment," and returned to his post, with an expressed readiness to retire any time, if the President felt that such retirement would promote the success of the Administration.

"The untrained diplomatist of Illinois," declare Nicolay and Hay, "had thus met and conjured away, with unsurpassed courage and skill, one of the severest crises that ever threatened the integrity of his Administration. He had to meet it absolutely unaided; from the nature of the case he could take no advice from those who were nearest him in the Government. By his bold and original expedient of confronting the senators with the Cabinet, and having them discuss their mutual misunderstandings under his own eye, he cleared up many dangerous misconceptions, and as usually happens when both parties are men of intelligence and good will, brought about a friendlier and more considerate feeling between his Government and the Republican leaders than had ever before existed. By placing Mr. Chase in such an attitude that his resignation became necessary to his own sense of dignity Lincoln made himself master of the situation; by treating the resignations and the return to the Cabinet of both ministers as one and the same transactions, he saved for the nation the invaluable services of both, and preserved his own position of entire impartiality between the two wings of the Union party."

Lincoln's magnanimity was constantly shown by the absence of all personal feeling when it became necessary for him to decide public questions or to

make important appointments. Edwin M. Stanton
did not belong to his political party and did not vote
for him as President. He had received scant courtesy
at Stanton's hands, when they first met in Cincinnati
as associate counsel in the historic "Reaper Case."
After Lincoln became President, Stanton was unsparing and abusive in his criticism, often referring to him
and his Administration in terms of contempt. Notwithstanding all this, Lincoln did not hesitate to invite him into his official family to fill the exceedingly
important post of Secretary of War, made vacant by
the resignation of Secretary Cameron.

Knowing the forcefulness of Stanton's great personality, his firmness, which sometimes developed into
obstinacy, and his lack of tact in dealing with others,
some of Lincoln's friends were greatly alarmed at
his appointment, warned the President that nothing
could be done with him, and predicted that he "would
run away with the whole concern." To this expression of alarm, Lincoln is said to have replied: "We
may have to treat him as they are sometimes obliged
to treat a Methodist minister I know of out West.
He gets wrought up to so high a pitch of excitement
in his prayers and exhortations, that they are obliged
to put bricks into his pockets to keep him down. We
may be obliged to serve Stanton in the same way, but
I guess we'll let him jump a while first."

It was inevitable that differences of opinion should
arise between men who were so unlike in their temper-
aments as Lincoln and Stanton. But the fact that
both of them were passionately devoted to the Union

and were united in a common purpose with the same
end in view, usually made it possible for them to work
together in harmony. Sometimes Stanton lost his temper and made unkind remarks about his Chief, but
Lincoln's inexhaustible patience and never-failing
good humor enabled him to ignore these ill-natured
outbursts and to hold his attention to the main issue.
Even when it was reported to him that Stanton had
called him a fool, he good-naturedly replied that if
Stanton said that, he supposed it must be true, for
Stanton was nearly always right.

Stanton was given the largest liberty in the conduct
of the affairs of his department and had the full confidence and the loyal support of the President, who
frequently defended his Secretary against the bitter
attacks which were made upon him, sometimes assum-
ing personal responsibility for acts which were the subject of the criticism.

There was, however, a limit to Lincoln's forbearance.
When necessary, he did not hesitate to act with promptness and with a finality that once for all settled an
important issue or forever put an end to unnecessary
quibbling. A most impressive illustration of this is
found in the lecture which he read to his Cabinet when
he was convinced that a movement was on foot to force
one of their number to resign:

> "I must myself be the judge how long to retain in,
> and when to remove any of you from his position. It
> would greatly pain me to discover any of you endeavor-
> ing to procure another's removal, or in any way to
> prejudice him before the public. Such endeavor would

be a wrong to me, and much worse, a wrong to the country. My wish is that on this subject no remark be made, nor question asked by any of you, here, or elsewhere, now, or hereafter."

But the test of Lincoln's patience and forbearance was not by any means confined to his experiences with generals and Cabinet members. He had to contend constantly with disturbing influences which were in no way officially connected with his Administration. One of the most annoying of these influences centered in the public press of which the *New York Tribune* was the most influential representative. Its editor, Horace Greeley, was a man of unique character. His ability was unquestioned. His motives were, in the main, good. But his impulses sometimes overpowered his judgment, and his eccentricities were so marked as to make it exceedingly difficult to retain his good will and support without surrendering to his dictation, which was not infrequently the result of his prejudice.

In the months which intervened between the election and the inauguration of Lincoln, when he was passing through the severe ordeal of witnessing the organized preparation to destroy the Union which he was hoping and planning to save when he became President, Greeley was publishing editorials in which he contended that if certain states wanted to go out of the Union, they should be permitted to do so. While this "dangerous and illogical" policy was in direct opposition to Lincoln's views and greatly increased the burden of anxiety which he was carrying, he nevertheless made no reply.

Under date of August 20, 1862, *The Tribune* published an editorial entitled "The Prayer of 20,000,000." This "Open Letter" to President Lincoln charged him with failure to execute the laws already enacted against slavery, and of being "unduly influenced by the counsels, the representations, the menaces of certain fossil politicians hailing from the border slave States." This unwarranted attack came at a most critical time in the progress of the war, when the patient President was bending every energy to hold the "Border States" in the Union, and was awaiting a Union victory before making public his Emancipation Proclamation, which had been prepared and submitted to his Cabinet for their consideration nearly a month before. On August 22, he replied in an "Open Letter" which, while most magnanimous in spirit, was so forceful in its logic as to nullify the effects of the false charges and insinuations made against him and his Administration.

The summer of 1864 was crowded with trouble for President Lincoln. Constant criticism poured in upon him. By some, he was severely arraigned for the continuation of the war. Others denounced him for using all the means at his command to hasten the end. Not a few were for peace at any price, and therefore ready to give friendly consideration to any suggestion looking to that end. Prominent among them was Greeley, who transmitted to the President a letter from an irresponsible individual by the name of Jewett, who claimed to have authority for stating that two ambassadors representing the Southern Confederacy were in Canada with full powers to negotiate for peace.

With this letter was enclosed one of his own in which he declared that there existed "a widespread conviction that the government and its prominent supporters are not anxious for peace, and do not improve proferred opportunities to achieve it." Following this unwarranted attack, it was urged that overtures for peace be made.

While Lincoln had no faith in Jewett's proposal, he promptly proceeded to act upon Greeley's urgent request that it be given consideration, by replying to his letter under date of July 9, 1864:

> "If you can find any person, anywhere, professing to have any proposition of Jefferson Davis in writing, for peace, embracing the restoration of the Union and abandonment of slavery, whatever else it embraces, say to him he may come to me with you; and that if he really brings such proposition, he shall at the least have safe conduct with the paper (and without publicity, if he chooses) to the point where you shall have met him. The same if there be two or more persons."

This frank reply greatly embarrassed Greeley, as it made him responsible for carrying out his own request. Instead of acting, he continued to write letters. Finally the correspondence was ended by a telegram from the President, dated July 15, 1864: "I suppose you received my letter of the 9th. I have just received yours of the 13th, and am disappointed by it. I was not expecting you to send me a letter, but to bring me a man, or men. Mr. Hay goes to you with my answer to yours of the 13th."

The letter referred to bore the same date as the telegram and read:

"Yours of the 13th is just received, and I am disappointed that you have not already reached here with those commissioners, if they would consent to come on being shown my letter to you of the 9th instant. Show that and this to them, and if they will come on the terms stated in the former, bring them. I not only intend a sincere effort for peace, but I intend that you shall be a personal witness that it is made."

No longer able to evade responsibility, Greeley reluctantly went to Niagara, where he learned that the alleged commissioners were without authority to act and that their whole purpose was to deceive the people of the United States into thinking that President Lincoln had refused to consider an offer for peace. Unwilling to assume the blame for his own failure, his only defense was implied censure of the President, indicated by his persistence in insisting that he was determined to refuse all offers of peace.

Lincoln's opportunity for complete vindication came with a request that he permit the publication of the entire correspondence. To this request he readily acceded, with the one condition that a few passages from the Greeley letters be omitted, since he felt that their publication would have an injurious effect upon the Union cause because of the gloomy aspect which they disclosed. With characteristic obstinacy, Greeley insisted that his letters, if published at all, must be printed entire, and even declined the cordial invitation of the President—"Please come over and see me." The final outcome was that Lincoln dropped the matter and silently submitted to the continued misrepresentations which resulted. Not until after his death were all the facts made known by the publication of the entire correspondence.

In this whole proceeding is found another striking illustration of the magnanimity of the great President, who was ever ready to sacrifice himself, if he could thereby advance the cause to which his life was dedicated.

In fact, it was Lincoln's magnanimity, so constantly manifested in all the varied relations of his eventful life, that enabled him to evince that unlimited patience —to exercise that remarkable self-control, which was the secret of his control of all the turbulent factors with which he had constantly to contend. It was his magnanimity which made possible the realization of both his "oft-expressed personal wish that all men everywhere could be free" and also of his exalted purpose that "this nation under God shall have a new birth of freedom; and that government of the people, by the people, for the people shall not perish from the earth."

CHAPTER VIII

LINCOLN'S EDUCATION

"EDUCATION defective" is the second item of information contained in the brief reply of Abraham Lincoln, in June, 1858, to the request of the compiler of the *Dictionary of Congress* that he furnish a sketch of his life.

If defective education is a necessary result of extremely limited opportunities for going to school, there can be no doubt that Lincoln's education was, indeed, defective. How limited his opportunities were for securing formal schooling, we learn from his own statements.

In 1859, his friend, Jesse W. Fell, requested him to prepare a sketch of his life. With this request he complied. Along with the sketch, he sent a letter whose opening sentences are most characteristic:

"Herewith is a little sketch, as you requested. There is not much of it, for the reason, I suppose, that there is not much of me. If anything be made out of it, I wish it to be modest, and not to go beyond the material."

In this sketch he describes the schools of Spencer County, Indiana, where he lived from the time of the removal of his family from Kentucky in his eighth

year, until he was twenty-one, and comments upon his
lack of educational opportunity:

> "There were some schools, so called, but no qualifi-
> cation was ever required of a teacher beyond 'readin,'
> writin' and cipherin' ' to the rule of three. If a strag-
> gler supposed to understand Latin happened to so-
> journ in the neighborhood, he was looked upon as a
> wizard. There was absolutely nothing to excite ambi-
> tion for education. Of course, when I came of age I
> did not know much. Still, somehow, I could read,
> write, and cipher to the rule of three, but that was all.
> I have not been to school since. The little advance I
> now have upon this store of education, I have picked
> up from time to time under the pressure of necessity."

In 1860, at the request of another friend, he wrote
an autobiography to be used in the preparation of a
biography for the campaign which resulted in his nomination for the Presidency. This most interesting document accurately describes the important experiences
of his life from the time of his birth in 1809 up to and
including the political campaign of 1856, in which he
had a large part. It is written in the third person,
giving to the reader the impression that some one was
furnishing information about Abraham Lincoln.

"Before leaving Kentucky," we learn from this Autobiography, "he and his sister were sent, for short
periods, to A B C schools, the first kept by Zachariah
Riney, and the second by Caleb Hazel."

After recounting the incidents connected with the
removal of the family, in 1816, from Kentucky to Spencer County, Indiana, and relating some of the experi-

ences of life in the "unbroken forest,' 'the Autobiography again refers to his schooling as follows:

"While here, Abraham went to A B C schools by littles, kept successively by Andrew Crawford,—Sweeney, and Azel W. Dorsey. He does not remember any other. . . . Abraham now thinks that the aggregate of all his schooling did not amount to one year. He was never in a college or academy as a student, and never inside of a college or academy building till since he had a law license. What he has in the way of education he has picked up. After he was twenty-three and had separated from his father, he studied English Grammar— imperfectly, of course, but so as to speak and write as well as he now does. He studied and nearly mastered the six books of Euclid since he was a member of Congress. He regrets his want of education, and does what he can to supply the want."

As a rule education is obtained through the agency of formal schooling. Among the exceptions which prove this rule, none is more striking than the one furnished by Abraham Lincoln.

With only the most limited opportunities for securing an education in the regular way, he nevertheless succeeded in developing all his powers, physical, mental, and moral to an unusual degree. As a result he constantly exemplified in his life the characteristics which are universally considered evidences of education. Among these the most important is character. Character is the ultimate purpose of all true education. Character is the supreme test of all right education. In his transparent character, Lincoln literally fulfilled the requirements implied in the question of one of the

Hebrew prophets—"What doth the Lord require of thee, but to do justly, and to love mercy, and to walk humbly with thy God?" The preceding chapters furnish abundant proof that Lincoln possessed in an unusual degree all the elements which enter into strength and nobility of character.

Another evidence of education is ability to concentrate attention upon work to be done. This ability Lincoln constantly manifested in a marvelous manner. It is well described and forcefully illustrated in *Intimate Character Sketches of Abraham Lincoln,* by Henry B. Rankin, who knew Lincoln with an intimacy made possible by over four years of study with him in his law office. In the intensely interesting chapter on "Characteristic Moods of Lincoln," we read:

"The first to be mentioned, and by far the strongest and most difficult to interpret, or even penetrate, while he was under its control, was his power to concentrate strictly all his mental faculties on the task or purpose immediately before him. In this mood he was absolutely impenetrable to anything else, or by any other person. He was thoroughly oblivious to surroundings. Every faculty of this remarkable man, while in this mood, was focused upon the fact or problem before him, viewing it from all angles and endeavoring with the keenest logic and most fertile, truth-inspired imagination to solve any problem or settle any question of fact or duty which challenged his attention. No person or influence could distract or hasten any of his peculiar mental processes at such times.

"I could cite numerous times and circumstances illustrating this mood of Lincoln that came under my observation in Springfield. Those who knew him there, and were afterwards near him in Washington, with whom I have spoken of this mood, told me that this peculiar characteristic became more and more a fixed habit under the pressure of his Presidential duties. I will refer to one instance, and that on an occasion of much historical importance.

"During the last weeks of his residence in Springfield it was difficult for him to find any place where he could be free from the interruption of callers. His home, his office in the State House, or the State Library, afforded him no privacy by day or night. To avoid this, Mr. C. M. Smith, his brother-in-law, fitted up a room in the third story over his store for Lincoln's private use, which could be entered only through the private office of Mr. Smith, in the back part of his large storeroom. This arrangement was known by a limited few, and he was to be seen when there only by persons bringing a line to Mr. Smith by Herndon. It was in that room that he prepared his First Inaugural Address, and thither I was sent twice by Herndon with books and clippings which the latter, at Lincoln's request, had selected from the State Library, the law office, and Herndon's home library, for study before preparing that remarkable state paper. On my return the last time, Herndon asked me if any word was sent back. I replied that I had no message and was sure Lincoln had not seen me when I came in and placed the packages on the table before him, or when I left the room. To this he replied with a satisfied smile: 'That's what I expected; he wishes nothing now so much as to be left alone.'

"In this mood lay his remarkable capacity for that special study necessary during the first months of his official duties as President, covering, as it did, so many new executive functions and judicial fields whose problems he must solve for himself. In the later and more momentous years this mood fitted him finally to be master of all politicians and of most of the military men around him, and the equal of his best generals in outlining the strategy of campaigns during the closing years of the Civil War."

In his *Life of Lincoln*, Herndon relates that when Lincoln was ready to begin work on his Inaugural Address, he mentioned the books he wanted to consult and that the surprisingly short list included "Henry Clay's Great Speech Delivered in 1850; Andrew Jackson's proclamation against nullification; and a copy of the Constitution." In addition to this list, "he afterward called for Webster's reply to Hayne, a speech which he had read when he lived at New Salem, and which he always regarded as the grandest specimen of American oratory."

To study this Inaugural Address is to be profoundly impressed with the marvelous insight into the problem of free government that it reveals; with the perfect understanding that it exhibits of the meaning and significance of the fundamental principles upon which the Union was founded; and with the clear discernment that it shows of the difference between the true and false interpretation of the Constitution as related to the alleged right of secession.

The preparation of this Address, with only a few books to consult, and with no one to help or to advise, furnishes positive proof of Lincoln's unusual power to think and to concentrate his thought upon questions of momentous importance. This power was not by any means wholly due to native ability. Neither was it acquired incidentally or accidentally. All through his life he had schooled himself to think honestly, logically, and persistently until he reached a conclusion which, to his mind was final, because he believed that it was founded upon truth and justice. Whatever the task which confronted him, he always made the best preparation of which he was capable.

Early in his life he conceived the idea that knowledge is a source of power, and his hungry mind was ever on the alert to add to his meager supply. No difficulty was too great to overcome, if by overcoming it he could learn something of value. When a clerk in Offutt's store in New Salem, he made up his mind that he would like to study English grammar. The necessity of walking twelve miles to get a copy of Kirkham's Grammar to study did not discourage him. In a short time, with a few suggestive helps from Mr. Graham, the local school-teacher, he mastered its contents. Other books, borrowed from friends, were mastered in the same way, much of his studying being done at night by means of the light from the burning shavings in the historic "cooper shop," which is still standing on its original site at New Salem.

His ability to fix and hold his attention upon the subject under consideration was again clearly shown by his mastery, in six weeks, of a treatise on surveying, in order that he might avail himself of an appointment as deputy surveyor. So intense and persistent was his mental application in gaining this mastery, that his friends were greatly worried because of the fear that his strong body would not endure the strain to which it was subjected by his almost constant study.

Further evidence of Lincoln's education is found in his constant growth in knowledge and power. "He grew according to the need," declares Ralph Waldo Emerson, in his "Remarks at the Funeral Services held at Concord, April 19, 1865"; "his mind mastered the problem of the day; and as the problem grew, so did his comprehension of it."

Many well authenticated incidents could be cited to prove that he did, indeed, grow "according to the need," whether that need was related to his own development or to his direction of public affairs, civil or military. It will be recalled that in his Autobiography he directs attention to his study of Euclid after he served in Congress. In his historic "Interview" with the Reverend John P. Gulliver, published in *The Independent,* dated September 1, 1864, he explains what led to this study and indicates the benefit which he derived from it. In answer to the questions, "Did you not have a law education?" and "How did you prepare for your profession?" he replied:

"Oh, yes! I 'read law', as the phrase is; that is, I became a lawyer's clerk in Springfield, and copied tedious documents, and picked up what I could of law in the intervals of other work. But your question reminds me of a bit of education I had, which I am bound in honesty to mention. In the course of my law-reading I constantly came upon the word *demonstrate*. I thought, at first, that I understood its meaning, but soon became satisfied that I did not. I said to myself, 'What do I do when I *demonstrate* more than when I *reason* or *prove?* How does *demonstration* differ from any other proof?' I consulted Webster's Dictionary. That told of 'certain proof,' 'proof beyond the possibility of doubt'; but I could form no idea what sort of proof that was. I thought a great many things were proved beyond a possibility of doubt, without recourse to any such extraordinary process of reasoning as I understood 'demonstration' to be. I consulted all the dictionaries and books of reference I could find, but with no better results. You might as well have defined *blue* to a blind man. At last I said, 'Lincoln, you can never make a lawyer if you do not understand what *demonstrate* means'; and I left my situation in Springfield, went home to my father's house, and staid there till I could give any proposition in the six books of Euclid at sight. I then found out what 'demonstrate' means and went back to my law studies."

In solving the many difficult problems which presented themselves in connection with the prosecution of the Civil War, there were no precedents to guide, no rules to follow, and very little trustworthy advice to be had. Jealousy and envy were rife not only among the politicians but among the military leaders. Many crises arose in which Lincoln had to act entirely upon his own judgment and to assume alone the heavy responsibility which such action involved. One of the most severe of these crises related to General Grant, for whose removal there was an almost universal demand. It is said that in Congress at that time there was only one member of Lincoln's party who had either the desire or the courage openly to defend Grant against the bitter attacks made upon him.

But Lincoln had grown "according to the need." With all the power due to his mental concentration he had studied the difficult problem presented by the military situation, until he was absolutely certain as to what course he should pursue, and with that courage which always animated him when he knew what he ought to do, he did not hesitate to do it. He stood by General Grant. The manner in which he took this wise and brave stand is vividly shown by Colonel A. K. McClure in his *Lincoln and Men of War Times.*

"I did not know Grant," said he, "at that time; had neither partiality nor prejudice to influence my judgment, nor had I any favorite general who might be benefited by Grant's overthrow, but I shared the almost universal conviction of the President's friends that he could not sustain himself if he attempted to sustain Grant by continuing him in command. Looking solely to the interests of Lincoln, feeling that the tide of popular resentment was so overwhelming against Grant that Lincoln must yield to it, I had repeated conferences with some of his closest friends, including Swett and Lamon, all of whom agreed that Grant must be removed from his command, and complained of Lincoln for his manifest injustice to himself by his failure to act promptly in Grant's removal. So much

was I impressed with the importance of prompt action
on the part of the President, after spending a day and
evening in Washington, that I called on Lincoln at
eleven o'clock at night and sat with him alone until
after one o'clock in the morning. He was, as usual,
worn out with the day's exacting duties, but he did
not permit me to depart until the Grant matter had
been gone over and many other things relating to the
war that he wished to discuss. I pressed upon him
with all the earnestness I could command the immediate removal of Grant as an imperious necessity to
sustain himself. As was his custom, he said but little,
only enough to make me continue the discussion until
it was exhausted. He sat before the open fire in the old
Cabinet room, most of the time with his feet up on the
high marble mantel, and exhibited unusual distress at
the complicated condition of military affairs. Nearly
every day brought some new and perplexing military
complication. He had gone through a long winter of
terrible strain with McClellan and the army of the
Potomac; and from the day that Grant started on his
Southern expedition until the battle of Shiloh he had
had little else than jarring and confusion among his
generals in the West. He knew that I had no ends to
serve in urging Grant's removal, beyond the single
desire to make him be just to himself, and he listened
patiently.

"I appealed to Lincoln for his own sake to remove
Grant at once, and in giving my reasons for it I simply voiced the admittedly overwhelming protest from
the loyal people of the land against Grant's continuance

in command. I could form no judgment during the conversation as to what effect my arguments had upon him beyond the fact that he was greatly distressed at this new complication. When I had said everything that could be said from my standpoint, we lapsed into silence. Lincoln remained silent for what seemed a very long time. He then gathered himself up in his chair and said in a tone of earnestness that I shall never forget: *'I can't spare this man; he fights.'* That was all he said, but I knew that it was enough, and that Grant was safe in Lincoln's hands against his countless hosts of enemies. The only man in all the nation who had the power to save Grant was Lincoln, and he had decided to do it. . . . . I knew enough of Lincoln to know that his decision was final, and I knew enough of him also to know that he reasoned better on the subject than I did, and that it would be unwise to attempt to unsettle his determination. . . . Lincoln was wiser than all those around him, and he not only saved Grant, but he saved him by such well-concerted effort that he soon won popular applause from those who were most violent in demanding Grant's dismissal."

No one will ever know the full history of all the long days of ceaseless toil and anxious care and of the night vigils through which Lincoln passed in order that he might grow in comprehension as his problems grew in difficulty. We do know that because of his comprehension of both governmental and military affairs, his mind was able to master the problems of each succeeding day and then successfully solve them.

The power to think is intimately related to the power to express thought in simple, forceful language. The possession of this power is an evidence of education. The lack of such power is an indication of the lack of education. The ponderous style that sometimes characterizes expression is usually due to the insignificance of the thoughts that are expressed. Clear thinking invariably seeks expression in clear language. Just as Lincoln's thought was always marked by clearness and accuracy, so his expression of thought always conformed to the same standards. It is impossible to misunderstand his meaning, because his language, which is always the embodiment of simplicity, states exactly what his clear and accurate thinking prompted him to say.

His unusual ability to use the mother tongue with such simplicity, accuracy, and precision, like his unusual power to think so clearly and logically, was acquired by the most persistent self-schooling combined with the most laborious practice. The method by which he thus schooled himself is described in the Gulliver Interview previously referred to. In the opening paragraphs of this "Interview," Mr. Gulliver refers to the impression made upon him by the speech which he had heard Lincoln give the morning before at Norwich, Connecticut, and to his introduction to Lincoln at the railroad station, when waiting for the train. After boarding the train, they entered into a conversation in which Lincoln was asked to explain how he gained his "unusual power of putting things," the request being accompanied with the observation that "it must have been a matter of education," and the question, "What has your education been?" To this request Lincoln replied:

"Well, as to education, the newspapers are correct—I never went to school more than six months in my life. But, as you say, this must be a product of culture in some form. I have been putting the question you ask me, to myself, while you have been talking. I can say this, that, among my earliest recollections, I remember how, when a mere child, I used to get irritated when anybody talked to me in a way I could not understand. I don't think I ever got angry at anything else in my life. But that always disturbed my temper, and has ever since. I can remember going to my little bedroom, after hearing the neighbors talk of an evening with my father, and spending no small part of the night walking up and down, and trying to make out what was the exact meaning of some of their, to me, dark sayings. I could not sleep, though I often tried to, when I got on such a hunt after an idea, until I had caught it; and when I thought I had got it, I was not satisfied until I had repeated it over and over, until I had put it in language plain enough, as I thought, for any boy I knew to comprehend. This was a kind of passion with me, and it has stuck by me, for I am never easy now when I am handling a thought till I have bounded it north and bounded it south and bounded it east and bounded it west. Perhaps that accounts for the characteristic you observe in my speeches, though I never put the two things together before."

In this "Interview" are revealed the secrets of Lincoln's remarkable power in the use of language. In the first place, his desire to understand all that he heard was so intense that failure to realize this desire made him unhappy and even angry. It is interesting to try to imagine his childhood struggles in his lonely room, when on the hunt of an idea, determined to think out for himself the hidden meaning of some conversation to which he had listened. The final step in his process of self-education consisted of the persistent drill to which he subjected himself by bounding the "caught idea" north, east, south, and west and of calling to his aid every illustration or anecdote at his command which would enable him to tell what he had learned, with so much difficulty, to the other boys (and later on to the people of a nation) in such simple language as would make it perfectly plain to them. "Eloquent simplicity" characterized all that Lincoln said or wrote. His use of English well illustrates Emerson's definition—"Eloquence is the power to translate truth into language perfectly intelligible to the person to whom you speak."

Reading always has a large influence for good or ill upon character, thought, growth, and language. It is therefore both interesting and important to know what Lincoln read. It was Herndon's expressed belief that he "read less and thought more than any man in his sphere in America." This statement is probably true. The last half of it is certainly true. Fortunately, there is a reasonably accurate record of what he did read. In his boyhood home one book constituted the library. That book was the Bible. Other books which he read, aside from possibly a few textbooks of the most elementary character, were borrowed from friends and neighbors. It is believed that the first book he ever owned was the *Life of Washington* by Mason L Weems, who claimed to have been, at one time, the rector of Mount Vernon parish and thereby the spiritual adviser of Washington. The purchase of this book was a matter of necessity rather than choice. The story is that it was borrowed from Josiah Crawford, a close-fisted farmer of the neighborhood, by the youthful Lincoln, whose hunger to learn led him to read everything to be found within walking distance of his home. Having been left in a crack between two logs in the Lincoln cabin, the book was seriously damaged by rain. The damage was assessed at seventy-five cents, which the unfortunate borrower paid by "pulling fodder" for three days.

In his later life, even when he was President, he often referred to the impressions made upon his mind by reading this *Life of Washington* and "always contended that it was better for the young men of the country to regard Washington in the light of a demigod, as Parson Weems describes him, than to shake their faith in the greatest hero of American history by narrating his mistakes and follies as if he were a common man." This bit of philosophy is needed in these modern times when there seems to be a tendency to hunt for every indication of human weakness in the great men of the past, rather than to dwell upon the dominant qualities of their characters, which were in the main noble and true.

There is general agreement among Lincoln's reliable biographers that his early reading was largely confined to the Bible, Weems's *Life of Washiington,*

Aesop's Fables, Robinson Crusoe, Bunyan's *Pilgrim's Progress,* a *History of the United States* and the *Revised Statutes of Indiana,* which also contained a number of documents relating to the political history of the territory of Indiana, together with the Declaration of Independence and the Constitution of the United States.

It is definitely known that when Lincoln "kept store" at New Salem, he made good use of his leisure time in reading all the books he could secure. It was then that he became interested in Burns and Shakespeare, partly through the influence of Jack Kelso, a shiftless resident of the community, who knew and loved good literature and who spent most of his time loafing, fishing, and quoting from the books he had read. The taste thus acquired led Lincoln to a fair degree of familiarity with the writings of a number of English and American authors. That Shakespeare was his favorite is shown by the fact that he often quoted or read aloud from the tragedies and historical plays, *Hamlet, Macbeth,* and *Richard II* being his favorites. Carpenter, in his *Six Months at the White House,* quotes Lincoln as remarking—"It matters not to me, whether Shakespeare be well or ill acted; with him the thought suffices." He also relates a number of incidents which illustrate Lincoln's intimate knowledge of Shakespeare's plays and his remarkable interpretation of some of their most important passages.

Lincoln loved poems of a sad and reminiscent nature, such as "The Last Leaf" by Oliver Wendell Holmes and "Oh, Why Should the Spirit of Mortal Be

Proud?" by William Knox. Referring to the former,
Henry C. Whitney, his intimate friend and biographer
says: "Over and over again I have heard him repeat:

> 'The mossy marbles rest
> On the lips that he has prest
>   In their bloom;
> And the names he loved to hear
> Have been carved for many a year
>   On the tomb!'

and tears would come unbidden to his eyes, probably
at thought of the grave at Gentryville (his mother's)
or that in the bend of the Sangamon (Ann Rut-
ledge's)."

It was doubtless to the latter poem that reference is
made in Lincoln's historic letter of April 18, 1846, to
William Johnston, with whom he conducted a literary
correspondence which has recently attracted a great
deal of attention, and to whom he sent copies of his
own poems written after a visit to his boyhood home
at Gentryville, Indiana. In this letter he says:

> "I have not your letter now before me; but, from
> memory I think you ask me who is the author of the
> piece I sent you, and that you do so ask as to indicate a
> slight suspicion that I myself am the author. Beyond
> all question, I am not the author. I would give all I am
> worth, and go in debt, to be able to write so fine a piece
> as I think that is. Neither do I know who is the au-
> thor. I met it in a straggling form in a newspaper last
> summer, and I remember to have seen it once before,
> about fifteen years ago, and this is all I know about it."

Lincoln loved to repeat this poem to his friends, and
to the day of his death it remained his favorite. The

sentiment which it expresses is certainly in harmony with the spirit of humility which characterized his entire life.

The reading and study of law had a peculiar fascination for Lincoln and exercised a most potent influence on his education. The foundation of truth and justice, upon which law rests, appealed to his keen sense of right, just as the orderly, logical course of legal procedure appealed to his reason. His introduction to the study of law and government came before he moved from Gentryville, with the loan of the *Revised Statutes of Indiana,* a volume which contained other important documents such as the Declaration of Independence, the Constitution of the United States, and the Act for the Government of the Northwest Territory, one article of which provided that neither slavery nor involuntary servitude should exist except in punishment for crime. From the study of this book, Lincoln undoubtedly gained a comprehensive knowledge of the methods by which Indiana passed from a territory to a state and of the character of the laws which had been enacted for the government of the state; and what was of much greater importance, a true conception of the freedom from slavery to which the new state was dedicated, together with a clear understanding of the fundamental principles of government embodied in the Constitution of the United States.

After Lincoln had moved from Gentryville and entered upon his fateful business career in New Salem, an incident occurred which resulted in a revival of his interest in the study of law.

From a migrant, westward bound, he bought an old
barrel that had become an incumbrance to its owner,
who was glad to dispose of it for fifty cents. This
purchase, made with no other thought than that of
granting a favor, proved to be of great value to Lincoln
who, in cleaning out the barrel, found that it contained
a complete edition of *The Commentaries of Blackstone*,
the celebrated authority on English law. These Commentaries made an unusual appeal to Lincoln's alert
mind and were a large factor in his education. He
read them with consuming interest, which completely
absorbed his attention until, to use his own words,
he "devoured them."

In addition to ruggedness of character, ability to
concentrate attention, power to think clearly and logically and to express thought with simplicity, and an
ever-increasing desire to know, Lincoln possessed to
an unusual degree that refinement of spirit and gen-
tleness of manner which are always conclusive evidence of education. These qualities were not by any
means wholly natural. In fact, they were largely the
product of self-education and of persistent cultivation.
In his earlier years he had a tendency to indulge in
satire, and sometimes used his caustic wit in such a
way as to wound the feelings of the victims to whom
it was directed. He lampooned Josiah Crawford, for
whom he "pulled fodder" for three days to pay for the
damaged copy of Weems's *Life of Washington*, with
such effect as to make him ashamed to appear in public.

There is good reason to believe that this close-fisted
neighbor was not the only one who felt the sting of

Lincoln's ridicule. He soon became convinced, however, of the harmful results as well as of the unkindness of such practices and ceased to indulge in them. It is related that before he left Gentryville, he asked the pardon of all whom he had thus wronged. Certain it is that all his later life was characterized by kindness and generosity to both friend and foe. To his intimate friend, Joshua Speed, Lincoln is reported to have said in one of the many confidential talks they had:

"Speed, die when I may, I want it said of me by those who knew me best, that I always plucked a thistle and planted a flower where I thought a flower would grow."

His desire has been more than fulfilled. Not only those who knew him best but everywhere in the world people of all nations and tongues, who know him only as an historic figure, are to-day, more than ever before in the world's history, recognizing that true greatness is found only in the gentle and forgiving spirit upon which the enduring fame of Abraham Lincoln rests. Even in the heart of the interior of China, two thousand miles from the coast, can be found on the mud walls of the huts of the poorest people rude wood cuts of the man who, under God, helped to save a nation and emancipate a race—an illustration of the far-reaching effect of the great deeds of a great life dedicated to unselfish service.

Was Abraham Lincoln's "education defective"? Measured by the conventional standards of society it was. But if education is to be measured by ability to think profoundly upon the greatest problems of both individual and national life; to state clearly and force-fully the results of such thinking in language whose beauty and simplicity still charm the entire world; to feel so deeply the wrongs of an enslaved race that life becomes one constant struggle for their freedom; to perform such heroic deeds of exalted patriotism as inspired the loyal people of a divided country to fight on through four years of Civil War to win a victory which forever settled the question of national su-premacy; to conduct that war in such a magnanimous spirit as to leave no cause for bitterness in the hearts of the vanquished; to win the esteem and reverence of the poorest people living in regions far removed from civilization; to live a personal life so clean and pure and wholesome that all admire and none criticise—if these achievements be the test of education, rather than the formal standards of society and schools, then there can be no doubt that Abraham Lincoln was one of the most thoroughly educated men the world has ever known.

CHAPTER IX

LINCOLN'S GETTYSBURG ADDRESS

NESTLED among the hills of southern Pennsylvania, near the Maryland border, is the little town of Gettysburg, known to-day all over the world as the scene of the greatest battle ever fought on American soil—the decisive battle of the Civil War. There, amidst the heat of the first three days of July, 1863, nearly two hundred thousand men, composed of the Blue of the Union forces and the Gray of the Southern Confederacy—all Americans —were engaged in a death grapple which was to decide the fate of the Nation. When the Fourth of July, the birthday of that Nation dawned, it was known that the victory for national supremacy had been won at a terrible cost, for many thousands of the bravest men who had ever lived and fought were numbered among the dead and wounded.

To Andrew G. Curtin, the great war governor of Pennsylvania, who visited the battle-field shortly after the battle of Gettysburg for the purpose of bringing relief to the sick and wounded soldiers, and to David Wills, a resident of the town and the chosen personal representative of the Governor, is due the credit of proposing the establishment of the Gettysburg National Cemetery. By the authority of Governor Curtin, Mr. Wills invited the different states whose soldiers had lost their lives in the battle to co-operate in removing their remains from the hastily made graves in which they had been, in many instances, only partially buried, to a cemetery, the grounds for which he had purchased, at the request of the Governor, to be paid for by the state of Pennsylvania. The grounds thus purchased consisted of about seventeen acres located on Cemetery Hill and overlooking the entire battlefield.

The invitation extended to the various states to co-operate in this patriotic service was cordially accepted, and in a comparatively short time the cemetery grounds were laid out with plots assigned to each of the loyal states whose soldiers had fallen in the battle. The official list published in 1865 by the state of Pennsylvania, shows that 3,555 soldiers are buried in this cemetery.

Even before the close of the war, a movement was started to preserve the existing memorials of the great battle, and on April 30, 1864, the Gettysburg Battle-Field Memorial Association was incorporated by an act of the Legislature of Pennsylvania. The object of this Association was declared to be "to hold and preserve the battle-grounds of Gettysburg, on which were fought the actions of the first, second, and third days of July, one thousand eight hundred and sixty-three, with the natural and artificial defenses as they were at the time of said battle, and by such perpetuation, and such memorial structures as a generous and patriotic people may aid to erect, to commemorate the heroic deeds, the struggles and the triumphs of their brave defenders."

Too great praise cannot be given to the officers, members, and friends of this Memorial Association, who for thirty years devoted much time and effort to directing the work of surveying the grounds, locating and laying out roads and avenues, and providing for the erection of suitable memorials and monuments. The revenues of the Association were not sufficient to meet the large demands made upon it, and in 1891 a committee was appointed to devise a plan for the future maintenance of the battle-field. As a result of the efforts and the recommendations of this committee, on March 3, 1893, the Congress of the United States passed an act authorizing the Secretary of War to appoint a commission of three members to have charge of the work of preserving the battle lines at Gettysburg. On February 11, 1895, Congress passed another act to establish a National Military Park at Gettysburg. Under the provisions of this act, the work has gone forward until to-day the "Gettysburg National Park," containing about twenty-five square miles, is the best preserved and the most widely known battle-field in the world.

The act provided that a bronze tablet should be erected, containing on it a medallion likeness of President Lincoln and the Address delivered by him on the occasion of the dedication of the national cemetery at Gettysburg. The form of the Address which appears on the tablet as prescribed by Congress, is that of the final revision made by Lincoln:

"Four score and seven years ago our fathers brought forth on this continent a new nation, conceived in liberty and dedicated to the proposition that all men are created equal.

"Now we are engaged in a great civil war, testing whether that nation, or any nation so conceived and so dedicated, can long endure. We are met on a great battlefield of that war. We have come to dedicate a portion of that field as a final resting place for those who here gave their lives that that nation might live. It is altogether fitting and proper that we should do this.

"But, in a larger sense, we cannot dedicate, we cannot consecrate, we cannot hallow this ground. The brave men, living and dead, who struggled here, have consecrated it far above our poor power to add or detract. The world will little note, nor long remember what we say here; but it can never forget what they did here. It is for us, the living, rather to be dedicated here to the unfinished work which they who fought here have thus far so nobly advanced. It is rather for us to be here dedicated to the great task remaining before us; that from these honored dead we take increased devotion to that cause for which they gave the last full measure of devotion; that we here highly resolve that these dead shall not have died in vain; that this nation, under God, shall have a new birth of freedom, and that government of the people, by the people, for the people, shall not perish from the earth."

This action of Congress in providing for the erection of a tablet to contain the Gettysburg Address and specifying the exact form in which it was to be recorded is without precedent or parallel, and serves as a fitting climax to the interest which centers about that historic nineteenth of November, 1863, on which this remarkable Address was delivered.

It is exceedingly unfortunate that so many false statements relating both to its preparation and to the effect produced upon the people who heard it, should have gained such wide credence. It is most desirable that the facts connected with such an important event should be known.

In order that the proper historic setting for this may be given, it is necessary to go back to August 17, 1863. In a letter of that date Mr. Wills suggested to Governor Curtin that the Gettysburg Cemetery should be "consecrated by appropriate ceremonies." This suggestion met with the hearty approval of the Governor, who united with the governors of the other states having soldiers who fell in the ranks at Gettysburg, in a request that Mr. Wills make the necessary arrangements for the ceremonies. In accordance with this request, on September 23, 1863, Mr. Wills wrote the Honorable Edward Everett, of Massachusetts, inviting him to deliver the oration and naming October 23 as the date. On September 26 Mr. Everett replied to this invitation in a letter which is full of interest and which plainly shows a full realization of both the opportunity and the responsibility which came with an acceptance of the invitation:

"I have received your favor of the 23rd instant," he wrote, "inviting me, on behalf of the governors of the states interested in the preparation of a cemetery for the soldiers who fell in the great battles of July last, to deliver an address at the consecration.

I feel much complimented by this request, and would cheerfully undertake the performance of a duty at once so interesting and honorable. It is, however, wholly out of my power to make the requisite preparation by the 23rd of October. I am under engagements which will occupy all my time from Monday next to the twelfth of October, and, indeed, it is doubtful whether, during the whole month of October, I shall have a day at my command.

"The occasion is one of great importance, not to be dismissed with a few sentimental or patriotic commonplaces. It will demand as full a narrative of the events of the three important days as the limits of the hour will admit, and some appropriate discussion of the political character of the great struggle, of which the battle of Gettysburg is one of the most momentous incidents. As it will take me two days to reach Gettysburg, and it will be highly desirable that I should have at least one day to survey the battle-field, I can not safely name an earlier time than the 19th of November.

"Should such a postponement of the day first proposed be admissible, it will give me great pleasure to accept the invitation."

On November 2, Mr. Wills sent the following invitation to President Lincoln:

"The several states having soldiers in the Army of the Potomac, who were killed at the battle of Gettysburg, or have since died at the various hospitals which were established in the vicinity, have procured grounds on a prominent part of the field for a

Four score and seven years ago our fathers brought
forth, upon this continent, a new nation, conceived
in liberty, and dedicated to the proposition that
"all men are created equal"

Now we are engaged in a great civil war, testing
whether that nation, or any nation so conceived,
and so dedicated, can long endure. We are met
on a great battle field of that war. We have
come to dedicate a portion of it, as a final resting place for those who died here, that the nation
might live. This we may, in all propriety do. But, in a
larger sense, we can not dedicate— we can not
consecrate— we can not hallow, this ground—
The brave men, living and dead, who struggled
here, have hallowed it, far above our poor power
to add or detract. The world will little note, nor long
remember what we say here; while it can never
forget what they did here.
It is rather for us, the living, we here be dedica
to the great tasks here,

FIRST DRAFT OF LINCOLN'S GETTYSBURG ADDRESS
Photograph from original in Library of Congress—reduced.

ted to the great task remaining before us—
that, from these honored dead we take increased devotion to that cause for which
they here, gave the last full measure of devotion— that we here highly resolve these
dead shall not have died in vain; that
the nation, shall have a new birth of freedom, and that government of the people by
the people for the people, shall not perish from the earth.

LINCOLN'S GETTYSBURG ADDRESS—SECOND PAGE

cemetery, and are having the dead removed to them
and properly buried.   These grounds will be consecrated and set apart to this sacred purpose, by appropriate ceremonies, on Thursday, the 19th instant.
Honorable Edward Everett will deliver the oration.
I am authorized by the governors of the different
states to invite you to be present and participate in
these ceremonies, which will doubtless be very im-
posing and solemnly impressive.   It is the desire that
after the oration, you as Chief Executive of the nation, formally set apart these grounds to their sacred
use by a few appropriate remarks.   It will be a
source of great gratification to the many widows and
orphans that have been made almost friendless by
the great battle here, to have you here personally;
and it will kindle anew in the breasts of the comrades of these brave dead, who are now in the tented
field or nobly meeting the foe in the front, a confidence that they who sleep in death on the battle-
field are not forgotten by those highest in authority;
and they will feel that, should their fate be the same,
their remains will not be uncared for.   We hope you
will be able to be present to perform this last solemn
act to the soldier-dead on this battle-field."

Along with this official invitation, Mr. Wills sent
the following private note:

"As the hotels in our town will be crowded and
in confusion at the time referred to in the enclosed
invitation, I write to invite you to stop with me.   I
hope you will feel it your duty to lay aside pressing
business for a day to come on here to perform this

last sad rite to our brave soldier-dead on the 19th instant. Governor Curtin and Honorable Edward Everett will be my guests at that time, and if you come you will please join them at my house."

Business was, indeed, most pressing at that particular time. In addition to the heavy responsibilities connected with the Presidential office, especially in relation to the conduct of the war, a very important message must be prepared to send to Congress, which would soon meet. Notwithstanding this, the great-souled President, with his heart full of gratitude to all who had helped to win the victory at Gettysburg, promptly accepted both the official invitation, formally to set apart the grounds to their sacred use by a few appropriate remarks, and the private invitation to be a guest in the home of Mr. Wills. Because of the acceptance of the latter, the "Wills House" is one of the most interesting places in Gettysburg, while the "few appropriate remarks" made in response to the former, have "given to Gettysburg another claim to immortality and to American eloquence its highest glory."

Two brief letters relating to the journey to Gettysburg are significant and interesting.

On November 17, the President wrote to Secretary of the Treasury Chase:

"I expected to see you here at Cabinet meeting, and to say something about going to Gettysburg. There will be a train to take and return us. The time for starting is not yet fixed; but when it shall be I will notify you."

On the same date, Secretary of War Stanton sent the following characteristic note to President Lincoln outlining the arrangements he had made for the journey:

"It is proposed by the Baltimore and Ohio Road: First, to leave Washington, Thursday morning at 6 A.M. Second to leave Baltimore at 8 A.M., arriving at Gettysburg at twelve, noon, thus giving two hours to view the ground before the dedication ceremonies commence. Third, to leave Gettysburg at 6 P.M. and arrive at Washington at midnight, thus doing all in one day." Upon this note President Lincoln wrote an endorsement as characteristic of him as the note, itself, was of Secretary Stanton:

"I do not like this arrangement. I do not wish to so go that by the slightest accident we fail entirely; and at the best, the whole to be a mere breathless running of the gauntlet. But any way."

The plan was changed to suit the implied wishes of the President. At noon, November 18, the Presidential party started on its journey, reaching Gettysburg that evening. Only three members of the President's Cabinet were with him—Secretary of State Seward, Secretary of the Interior Usher, and Postmaster General Blair. Private secretaries Nicolay and Hay attended the President, who, upon arrival at Gettysburg, went at once to the home of Mr. Wills.

It is impossible to explain how the false statements relating to the preparation of the Gettysburg Address ever originated or to understand why these false statements were ever believed by thoughtful people. But even to this day, there are many who still persist in giving expression to the belief that this matchless oration simply sprang into existence, accidentally or incidentally, without any thought or preparation.

The following are examples of such statements which can be found in some of the so-called "Histories" and "Reminiscences" of Lincoln:

"President Lincoln while on his way from the capital to the battle-field was notified that he would be expected to make some remarks" and "retiring a short time," he prepared the Address.

"His remarks at Gettysburg were written in the car on his way from Washington to the battle-field upon a piece of pasteboard held on his knee."

"When the President rose to speak, he unpremeditately and solemnly said, 'It is intimated to me that this assemblage expects me to say something on this occasion.'"

The Perfect Tribute, by Mary Shipman Andrews, is one of the most beautiful stories in the entire realm of Lincoln literature. It richly deserves the wide reading which it has had, because it reveals in a marvelous manner the real spirit of President Lincoln as breathed in the Gettysburg Address. But it is unfortunate that it has been taken literally by many who have accepted, as being historically true, the statements relating to the preparation of this Address. President Lincoln did few, if any, of the things which the author of *The Perfect Tribute* credits him with doing on his way to Gettysburg. He did not gaze wistfully across the car at Edward Everett. That gentleman was not on the train, having gone to Gettysburg in advance by another route. He did not stretch out his long arm for the torn paper which Secretary Seward had thrown to the floor of the car, after opening a package of books, and ask if he might use it to do a little writing. But fully realizing that "the people had a right to the best he could give," he had not waited for the "leisure of the journey" to prepare, but had already thought out in a large measure, and had partially put in writing what he intended to say. That he "might give them his best," he had done what he had always done all his life with painstaking care, whenever he had an important duty to perform—he had made the most careful preparation. To presume that Abraham Lincoln could have done otherwise in meeting one of the most solemn and important obligations of his entire life is indeed an injustice to his memory.

No man in public life ever prepared with greater care what he had to say or exercised greater care in saying it than did Abraham Lincoln. Numerous incidents might be cited in proof of this. One directly connected with his visit to Gettysburg is sufficient. On the evening of the 18th of November a serenading party called on the different visitors of prominence for speeches. Several of them, including Secretary Seward, responded—some of them at considerable length. After repeated and persistent calls, President Lincoln appeared and said:

"I appear before you, fellow-citizens, merely to thank you for this compliment. The inference is a very fair one that you would hear me for a little while at least, were I to commence to make a speech. I do not appear before you for the purpose of doing so, and for several substantial reasons. The most substantial one of these is that I have no speech to make. In my position it is somewhat important that I should not say any foolish things. (A voice: 'If you can help it.') It very often happens that the only way to help it is to say nothing at all. Believing that is my present condition this evening, I must beg of you to excuse me from addressing you further."

Fortunately all the essential facts relating to the composition and delivery of the Address are available in an article furnished by Mr. Nicolay, President Lincoln's private secretary, who accompanied him on the trip to Gettysburg, and who presents abundant evidence to prove that he knows whereof he speaks. This article on "Lincoln's Gettysburg Address," published in the Century Magazine, volume 47, 1893-4, pages 596 to 608, is the original source of practically all the reliable information to be obtained on the subject of which it treats.

The following quotations from it are used with the special permission of The Century Company:

"There is neither record, evidence, nor well-founded tradition that Mr. Lincoln did any writing, or made any notes, on the journey between Washington and Gettysburg. The train consisted of four passenger coaches, and either composition or writing would have been extremely troublesome amid all the movement, the noise, the conversation, the

greetings, and the questionings which ordinary courtesy required him to undergo in these surroundings;
but still worse would have been the rockings and
joltings of the train, rendering writing virtually impossible.   Mr. Lincoln carried in his pocket the
autograph manuscript of so much of his address as
he had written at Washington the day before.   Pre-
cisely what that was the reader can now see by
turning to the facsimile reproduction of the original
draft, which is for the first time printed and made
public in this article.   It fills one page of the letter-
paper at that time habitually used in the Executive
Mansion, containing the plainly printed blank head-
ing; both paper and print giving convincing testimony to the simple and economical business methods then prevailing in the White House.

"The whole of this first page—nineteen lines—is
written in ink in the President's strong clear hand,
without blot or erasure; and the last line is in the
following form: 'It is rather for us the living to
stand here,' the last three words being, like the rest,
in ink.   From the fact that this sentence is incomplete, we may infer that at the time of writing it in
Washington the remainder of the sentence was also
written in ink on another piece of paper.   But when,
at Gettysburg on the morning of the ceremonies, Mr.
Lincoln finished his manuscript, he used a lead pencil, with which he crossed out the last three words of
the first page, and wrote above them in pencil 'we
here be dedica,' at which point he took up a new
half sheet of paper—not white letter-paper as be-

fore, but a bluish-gray foolscap of large size with wide lines, habitually used by him for long or formal documents, and on this he wrote, all in pencil, the remainder of the word, and of the first draft of the Address, comprising a total of nine lines and a half."

"The time occupied in this final writing was probably about an hour, for it is not likely that he left the breakfast table before nine o'clock, and the formation of the procession began at ten."

Concerning the preparation of the last page of the Address, Mr. Nicolay speaks with the authority of an eye witness, for in the same article, he says:

"It was after the breakfast hour on the morning of the 19th that the writer, Mr. Lincoln's private secretary, went to the upper room in the house of Mr. Wills which Mr. Lincoln occupied, to report for duty, and remained with the President while he finished writing the Gettysburg Address."

There can be no question, therefore, that the Gettysburg Address was carefully prepared and that no statements made by anyone to the contrary are worthy of any consideration.

In view of the fact that different versions of this Address are extant, it is highly important to know which is the correct one. Fortunately this was definitely settled by President Lincoln, himself, as related by Mr. Nicolay:

"Four days after Mr. Lincoln's return to Washington, Mr. Wills once more wrote him saying:

'On behalf of the States interested in the National Cemetery here, I request of you the original manu-

script of the dedicatory remarks delivered by you
here last Thursday. We desire them to be placed
with the correspondence and other papers connected
with the project.'

"To comply with this request, the President re-
examined his original draft, and the version which
had appeared in the newspapers, and saw that, because of the variations between them, the first
seemed incomplete, and the others imperfect. By
his direction, therefore, his secretaries made copies
of the Associated Press report, as it was printed in
several prominent newspapers. Comparing these
with his original draft, and with his own fresh
recollection of the form in which he delivered it, he
made a new autograph copy—a careful and deliberate revision—which has become the standard and
authentic text.

In making a comparison of the first draft of the
Address as the President wrote it and the Associated
Press report of its delivery, Mr. Nicolay notes the
following essential changes:

"1. The phrase, 'Those who died here,' was
changed to 'Those who here gave their lives.'

"2. The entire sentence, 'This we may in all propriety do,' was changed to 'It is altogether fitting
and proper that we should do this.'

"3. The sentence in the original draft, 'It is rather
for us the living we here be dedicated to the great
task remaining before us,' was transformed into two
sentences, thus: 'It is for us the living, rather to be
dedicated here to the unfinished work that they have

thus far so nobly carried on. It is rather for us to be here dedicated to the great task remaining before us.' .... The 'we' in the original was of course a mere slip of the pencil, 'to' having been intended.

"4. The phrase, 'Shall have a new birth of freedom,' was changed as follows: "Shall, under God, have a new birth of freedom.'

"The changes may have been prompted by the oratorical impulse of the moment; but it is more likely that in the interval of four hours occupied by coming to the grounds, and the delivery of Mr. Everett's oration, he (Lincoln) fashioned the phrases anew in his silent thought, and had them ready for use when he rose to speak.

"The other changes were merely verbal: as, 'have come' changed to 'are met'; 'a' changed to 'the'; 'for' changed to 'of'; 'the' changed to 'that'; 'hallowed' changed to 'consecrated'; the word 'poor' omitted; 'while' changed to 'but'; 'these' changed to 'that the'; 'government' changed to 'governments'; and the word 'and' interpolated in the last sentence. Most, if not all, of these are clearly errors of the shorthand."

Comparing the Associated Press Report with the final revision, Mr. Nicolay notes:

"That there were in all thirteen changes; that seven of these are a mere return to, or restoration of, words in the first draft, correcting the errors which evidently occurred in the transmission by telegraph and the newspaper typesetting, namely: 'are met' changed back to 'have come'; 'the' changed back to 'a'; 'of' changed back to 'for'; 'power' changed back to 'poor power'; 'the' changed back to 'these'; 'governments' changed back to 'government'; 'and' omitted from the last sentence, as at first.

"The other six changes are the President's own deliberate revision, namely: 'upon' changed to 'on'; 'it' changed to 'that field'; 'they have' changed to 'they who fought here have'; 'carried on' changed to 'advanced'; 'they here gave' changed to 'they gave'; and the phrase 'shall under God' transposed to read 'under God shall.' "

"In addition to that from Mr. Wills," says Mr. Nicolay, "other requests soon came to him for autograph copies. The number he made, and for what friends, cannot now be confidently stated, though it was probably half a dozen or more, all written by him with painstaking care to correspond word for word with his revision. If in any respect they differed from each other, it was due to accident and against his intention."

One of the "other requests" was from Mr. Everett himself, who wrote to President Lincoln on January 30, 1864:

"I shall have the honor of forwarding to you by express, to-day or on Monday next, a copy of the authorized edition of my Gettysburg Address and of the remarks made by yourself, and the other matters connected with the ceremonial of the dedication of the Cemetery. It appeared, owing to unavoidable delays, only yesterday.

"I have promised to give the manuscript of my address to Mrs. Governor Fish of New York, who is at the head of the Ladies' Committee of the Metropolitan fair. It would add very greatly to its value if I could bind up with it the manuscript of your dedicatory remarks, if you happen to have preserved it.

"I would further venture to request, that you would allow me also to bind up in the volume the very obliging letter of the 20th of November, 1863, which you did me the favor to write me. I shall part with it with much reluctance, and I shrink a little from the apparent indelicacy of giving some publicity to a letter highly complimentary to myself. But as its insertion would greatly enhance the value of the volume when sold at the fair, I shall, if I have your kind permission, waive all other considerations."

To this letter President Lincoln replied on February 4, 1864:

"Yours of January 30th was received four days ago; and since then the address mentioned has arrived. Thank you for it. I send herewith the manuscript of my remarks at Gettysburg, which, with my note to you of November 20th, you are at liberty to use for the benefit of our soldiers, as you have requested."

Leaves From Our Country's Authors is the title of a volume that was sold for the benefit of the soldiers at a fair held in Baltimore in April, 1864. This interesting volume of two hundred pages contained facsimile reproductions of writings from all the prominent American authors, and included the

Gettysburg Address, an autograph copy of which was furnished by President Lincoln at the verbal request of George Bancroft, the historian, who acted on behalf of the committee in charge of the publication. This copy was written on both sides of a letter sheet and could not be used for lithographing. On learning this, President Lincoln, with characteristic patience, made a second copy, generously permitting Mr. Bancroft to keep the first. The text of this copy is identical with that prescribed by Congress for use on the Tablet which has previously been referred to in this chapter.

The extreme importance of adhering to this standard text is forcefully presented by the late Major William H. Lambert in his scholarly discussion of "The Gettysburg Address—When Written, How Received, Its True Form," published in No. 4, Vol. 33, of *The Pennsylvania Magazine of History and Biography*.

"In an address so brief, but so momentous, every syllable tells; and though the differences between the final revision and the speech as actually delivered are few and seemingly immaterial, the changes intensify its strength and pathos and add to its beauty, and as so revised the speech cannot be too jealously preserved as the ultimate expression of the author's sublime thought. Increasing appreciation of Lincoln's character and of his fitness for the great work to which in the providence of God he was called, enhances the value of his every word; and surely the form by which he intended this utterance should be judged is that in which we should perpetuate the Gettysburg Address."

It is not uncommon to hear statements to the effect that the Gettysburg Address was accorded little attention at the time of its delivery and that those who heard it had no appreciation of its beauty or realization of its significance. It is even reported that Secretary Seward and Mr. Everett commented upon it at its close in a most uncomplimentary manner, agreeing that it was a disappointment and a failure, wholly unworthy of the President. Even had such views been held by these distinguished men, it is most unreasonable to presume that they would have given expression to them under the attendant circumstances. What Mr. Everett really thought of the Address was expressed in the following letter sent to President Lincoln at Washington the next day:

"Not wishing to intrude upon your privacy when you must be much engaged, I beg leave in this way to thank you very sincerely for your great thoughtfulness for my daughter's accommodation on the platform yesterday, and much kindness to me and mine at Gettysburg. Permit me also to express my great admiration of the thoughts expressed by you with such eloquent simplicity and appropriateness at the consecration of the cemetery. I should be glad if I could flatter myself that I came as near the central idea of the occasion in two hours as you did in two minutes. My son, who parted from me at

Baltimore, and my daughter concur in this statement."

To this fine compliment, President Lincoln, with
characteristic modesty, replied:

> "Your kind note of to-day is received. In our respec-
> tive parts yesterday, you could not have been excused
> to make a short address, nor I a long one. I am pleased
> to know that in your judgment the little I did say was
> not a failure."

Whatever others may have thought or said about
the Address, it is not at all probable that Lincoln,
himself, had any realization of its greatness at the
time of its delivery. In fact, there is good reason to
believe that he felt that it was a failure. That he
should so feel is in harmony with his humility, which
always led him to underestimate rather than to over-
estimate the importance of what he said or did. It
is reasonable to infer, however, that his careful revision of the Address later on, is an indication that he
had somewhat modified his own estimate of its value.

Many accounts of the manner in which the Address was delivered and of its effects upon the audience have been published. No one of these accounts
is more trustworthy than that prepared expressly
for the author, in 1913, the fiftieth anniversary of
the occasion, by the late Superintendent John Morrow of Allegheny, Pennsylvania. Because of Mr.
Morrow's unusual opportunity to see and hear all
that transpired, he was able to speak with authority
and accuracy. The following quotations are taken
from his account:

"It was my privilege to be present on that historic

occasion. Half a century, freighted with changes destined to bless mankind to the remotest generations, has come and gone, but no impression in all these changeful years comes back to me with such indelible clearness and freshness as the divinely inspiring events of November 19th, 1863.

"My friend, Dr. A. P. Garber, and I, through a great deal of tribulation, arrived in the little, old-fashioned town of Gettysburg early on the morning of November 19th. The Gettysburg of fifty years ago was very different from the Gettysburg of today. At that time, there was only one little, poorly equipped railroad, about thirty miles in length, leading into Gettysburg. This was a short branch running from Hanover Junction on the main line of the Pennsylvania railroad between Harrisburg and Baltimore. It had been put wholly out of commission by Lee's army under General Early and was still in very bad condition, so that it took us all night, from about five o'clock in the evening until seven the next morning, to cover those thirty miles. We found the old town swarming with strangers. They had been coming for several days, expecting to attend the dedication. That nineteenth of November was one of the most beautiful, sunshiny days that any one could desire. The sky was clear; the air was pure and bracing; but there was an atmosphere of stillness, suppressed sorrow, and grief that seemed to pervade the whole country. The people talked in subdued and plaintive tones. The irresistible feeling of the thousands present was that they were in the

LINCOLN MEMORIAL AT GETTYSBURG

At the right of the bust of Lincoln is the tablet bearing his Gettysburg Address; at the left is the tablet bearing David Wills' invitation to the President to make "a few appropriate remarks" at the dedication of the new National Cemetery.

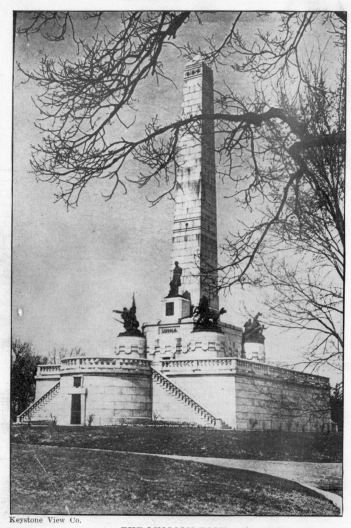

THE LINCOLN TOMB

In the crypt of this tomb, in Oak Ridge Cemetery, Springfield, Illinois,
lies the body of Abraham Lincoln.

midst of a great funeral concourse. Most of the
homes were elaborately draped in mourning and a
pall of sadness enveloped the entire community.

"The dedicatory exercises had been scheduled to
take place at one o'clock P.M. A large platform
about forty feet square had been erected at the
upper side of the cemetery, where the National Soldiers' Monument now stands. Doctor Garber and I
walked out there in the morning a little after eight
o'clock. We took seats on the front edge of the
platform and remained there until the dignitaries
arrived. We were then asked to slide down off the
platform, which we did, and stood on the ground,
leaning up against the front of it. Abraham Lincoln
and Edward Everett were shown to seats right in
front of where we stood. We were so close to them
that I could have touched either of them during the
entire dedicatory exercises. I heard all they said,
which was very little, while they sat there. Abraham Lincoln did not seem to be in a talkative mood.
Most of what he said was in answer to Everett's remarks about the pleasant weather, the great audience that had assembled there, and the gravity of
the occasion.

"A great choir of picked voices, assisted by the
Marine Band, furnished the music for the occasion.
The music was all of that minor order, dirge-like,
plaintive, and sorrowful. After two selections of
this character were rendered, Edward Everett, of
Massachusetts, was introduced. He was one of the
most polished and eloquent speakers in the United

States at that time. He was a graduate of the University, had studied theology and was ordained as a minister of the gospel, was elected Professor of Languages in Harvard University, served as a member of the United States Senate for a number of years, had been governor of Massachusetts, still later Secretary of State, and as a crowning recognition of his ability, was sent as Minister to England to represent the United States. It will, therefore, be seen that Edward Everett was eminently qualified by intellect, by education, and by experience to deliver such an address. He was a splendid looking man with fine physique, classical face, flowing hair, and impressive personality. I can see him still, as his majestic form appeared on that platform, the very embodiment of grace, dignity, polish, and eloquence itself. Every word he uttered, for perhaps two hours, was in the right place and correctly spoken. There was no hesitation from the beginning to the end of his oration. It was a masterpiece of history, rhetoric, literature, and logic and was delivered with an eloquence and sublimity that has rarely ever been equaled.

"When Everett sat down, there was a tumult of applause which lasted for some time. When the audience became somewhat settled, one of those pathetic pieces of music was rendered, and Abraham Lincoln was introduced. Lincoln was tall, six feet four inches in height, lank, and rather awkward looking in appearance. The strenuous labor of his early life had drawn his shoulders forward until he appeared stooped. The weight of responsibilities, past and present, had put deep furrows in his face. He rose from where he was sitting at the front of the platform and took out of his side pocket a sheet of paper on which his address was written. A great deal has been said, both in print and from the rostrum, about this paper's being untidy. I wish to state at this point, with all the positiveness of speech at my command, that these statements are untrue. The paper was clean and tidy and written with ink and not with pencil. It had been neatly folded and was in no way crumpled. I know these particulars to be true, for I was close enough to see, scarcely two feet away from Lincoln at the time he read the paper. He was deeply affected and stood there before that immense audience and gazed out over that great battle-field. His face assumed a sorrowful expression which I shall always remember. His mouth twitched, the muscles of his face seemed drawn, his cheeks were blanched, his chest heaved; he was overwhelmed with emotion and could not say a word. After what seemed a long time, the large tears began to steal their way down his cheeks, and when he had somewhat recovered his powers of expression, he commenced in tremulous tones to read those sublime sentences that he called his 'lines.' There was enough wisdom in those lines for half a dozen orations. These lines are said to have been translated into more foreign languages than any other address ever delivered in this country. With great effort he choked down his grief, while he read in a broken and quivering voice what he had written, and by the time he had partially recovered from his emotion, the lines were done and he sat down amidst a death-like stillness and silence. Edward Everett reached out his hand to him and said, 'Mr. Lincoln, allow me to congratulate you on those noble sentiments.' Lincoln replied, 'Dear me, Mr. Everett, I am sorry I could say so little. I had only twenty lines.' 'Yes, Mr. Lincoln, but there was more in your twenty lines than was in my twenty pages.' Their conversation continued and Everett made two or three attempts to cheer Lincoln by complimenting his address. But Lincoln warded him off each time and finally said, 'We shall try not to talk about my address. I failed! I failed! And that is about all that can be said about it.'

"It will no doubt be remembered that it has been said to the disparagement of Lincoln that Everett received all the applause and that Lincoln got none. While this is true, there never was an occasion where applause would have been more out of place than for Lincoln's address. His performance was essentially different from that of Everett's. In sentiment, in delivery, and in pathetic feeling, it was directed to the emotions, while Edward Everett's address was directed wholly to the intellect. To Abraham Lincoln that was a great funeral occasion, and as such he intuitively treated it. A prayer meeting or a funeral service is no place for applause, however eloquent the speaker may be. Lincoln's dramatic effort was a piece of pathetic feeling. It stirred up the elements of sorrow from center to circumference of the human soul. The difference between those two addresses may be stated in a few words. Edward Everett left that audience wreathed in smiles and in an outburst of admiration. Abraham Lincoln left it in tears. Edward Everett tickled the ear while Abraham Lincoln touched the heart. The one address called for prolonged applause while the other caused the audience to bow their heads in sorrow."

In the first chapter of this volume, attention is called to the tribute paid by the faculty of Oxford University to the beauty of Lincoln's language as contained in the letter to Mrs. Bixby. No finer tribute to his eloquence can be found than in the sentiment expressed by the late Lord Curzon in an address delivered by him to the students of Cambridge University, on "Modern Oratory":

"The finest speech in English of the last half century was delivered at Gettysburg—a speech made by a man who had been a country farmer and a district lawyer, which ranks among the glories and the treasures of mankind. I escape the task of deciding which is the masterpiece of British eloquence by awarding the prize to Abraham Lincoln.

CHAPTER X

THE LINCOLN TOMB

ON Lincoln's journey to Washington to assume his duties as President, those in charge of the Presidential party were informed that an attempt would be made to assassinate him in Baltimore, through which his train was scheduled to pass, February 23, on its way from Harrisburg to the national Capital. The information was furnished by reliable detective agencies, after careful investigation. At Philadelphia, Frederick W. Seward presented to Lincoln a special letter from his father, William H. Seward, who was to enter the Cabinet as Secretary of State. This letter inclosed the report of government detectives to General Winfield Scott, which report verified the information previously received in relation to the imminent danger of passing through Baltimore on the announced schedule and suggested that all risk might be avoided by so changing the plans that the President-elect would travel through Baltimore by night, without previous notice.

A council of a few of Lincoln's most intimate and trusted friends was held at Harrisburg to consider what should be done in the crisis. After careful deliberation it was agreed that the suggested change in

plans should be made. As a result, Lincoln and Colonel Ward H. Lamon, his long-time friend, left Harrisburg on the evening of February 22 and traveled by
special coach to Philadelphia, where berths had been
reserved for them on the midnight train from New
York to Washington. At 6:00 A.M., February 23,
they arrived safely at Washington.

All through his Presidency, Lincoln's life was repeatedly threatened by those who had some imaginary
grievance or who were not in sympathy with his persistent opposition to the extension of slavery. He
recognized the dangers that surrounded him and was
not indifferent to them. But knowing that in his own
heart there existed no ill will, even to his enemies, he
could not believe that any one could harbor political
hatred that would find expression in murder. Then,
too, he felt that it would be impossible to provide protection against all possible attempts to take his life,
"unless," as he quaintly expressed it, "he were to shut
himself up in an iron box, in which condition he could
scarcely perform the duties of a President."

He therefore went about his daily duties with little
or no protection, passing through the four years of
Civil War and the hatreds generated by it, unharmed.
But in the hour of approaching triumph for the cause
which he had so successfully defended, when his ten-
der heart was filled with joy that the long struggle was
about over and that peace was near at hand, and his
great mind was planning for the most magnanimous
treatment of his "dissatisfied fellow-countrymen," to
whom he had so earnestly and lovingly appealed in his

First Inaugural Address, he was stricken down by the assassin's bullet.

John Wilkes Booth, the assassin, was the leader of a small band who frequently met at a boarding house kept by Mrs. Mary E. Surratt, in Washington, where the crime was planned. He was an egotistical fanatic, bitterly disappointed at the re-election of President Lincoln and the surrender of the Army of Virginia at Appomattox. At one time he is reported to have conceived a plan to kidnap the President and take him to Richmond. He was a source of annoyance at the inauguration and is reported to have remarked that "he lost an excellent chance of killing the President that day."

In the Herndon-Weik *Life of Lincoln*, Frederick Stone, the counsel for one of Booth's accomplices, is quoted as stating that the immediate cause of the terrible crime was the sentiments expressed in the President's Last Public Address, April 11, 1865, relative to conferring, to a limited extent, the elective franchise upon the colored race on the basis of intelligence and military service. But whatever the cause which incited the act, with cruel and inexcusable hatred, he deliberately planned and maliciously executed one of the most brutal crimes in the world's history—a crime which instantly removed from the scene of action Abraham Lincoln, the best friend of the South as well as of the North, in whose great heart "there was no room for the memory of a wrong"—a crime which will forever associate the name of John Wilkes Booth with disgrace and infamy.

At twenty minutes past ten o'clock of the night of April 14, 1865, the fatal bullet was fired into the brain of the great President, as he sat with Mrs. Lincoln and two friends whom she had invited to join her, in a box at Ford's Theater, intent upon securing a little relaxation from the strenuous duties which so constantly claimed his time and strength.

"The wound would have brought instant death to most men," we read in the Nicolay and Hay *Life of Lincoln,* "but his vital tenacity was extraordinary. He was, of course, unconscious from the first moment; but he breathed with slow and regular respiration throughout the night. As the dawn came, and the lamplight grew pale in the fresher beams, his pulse began to fail; but his face even then was scarcely more haggard than those of the sorrowing group of statesmen and generals around him. His automatic moaning, which had continued throughout the night, ceased; a look of unspeakable peace came upon his worn features. At twenty-two minutes after seven he died. Stanton broke the silence by saying, 'Now he belongs to the ages.' Dr. Gurley kneeled by the bedside and prayed fervently. The widow came in from the adjoining room, supported by her son, and cast herself with loud outcry on the dead body."

The tragic death scene occurred in the house owned by William Peterson, and located at 516 Tenth Street, just opposite Ford's Theater. The President was removed there at the direction of the physician in charge, as it would have been impossible to take him to the White House over the (then) rough streets without bringing on a fatal hemorrhage. It is sad, indeed, to recall that this head of a great government, master of men, and emancipator of a race, who was born in a rude cabin which could scarcely be called a home, was not even permitted to die at home—the official home provided for the Presidents of the nation that he had done so much to save.

It is fitting, however, that the house where his earthly life ended should become a sacred Lincoln shrine. Lovers of Lincoln, visiting the building, reverently pause awhile in the room where he died, and appreciatively study the "Oldroyd Lincoln Memorial Collection," gathered through many years of painstaking care and loving service by Mr. O. H. Oldroyd, whose volumes—*The Assassination of Abraham Lincoln* and *The Poets' Lincoln* are both valuable contributions to Lincoln literature.

In the North, with few exceptions, the grief due to President Lincoln's death was as genuine as it was universal. The people of the South also shared, in a measure, in the sorrow; for down in their hearts they could not help feeling that he had never borne them any ill will. Perhaps, they may have realized to some extent what he would have done to "bind up the Nation's wounds," could he have lived to guide the work of reconstruction "with malice toward none and charity for all."

In the nation's capital, rejoicing at the prospects of the near approach of peace was suddenly turned into the deepest mourning. Public buildings and business houses and homes of all types, of the poor as well as of the rich, were alike draped with the emblems of sorrow, which centered in the White House where, silent in death, lay the body of the martyred President.

On the following Wednesday, April 19, funeral services were held in the historic East Room of the White House. They were fittingly characterized by brevity and simplicity, under the direction of Bishop Simpson of the Methodist Church and Dr. Gurley of the New York Avenue Presbyterian Church, in which President Lincoln and his family were regular worshippers. At the close of these services, the body was removed to the rotunda of the Capitol in a magnificent funeral car, accompanied by a vast procession, at the head of which marched a detachment of colored troops. There, all through the remainder of the day and all of the night of the 19th, and until the evening of the 20th, it rested, while thousands of deeply sympathizing friends reverently passed to pay their tribute of love to the one whose death had so profoundly stirred their hearts.

At eight o'clock on Friday morning, April 21, the funeral train started on its long, sad journey to Springfield where a little more than four years before the loved Lincoln had bidden farewell to his friends and neighbors. For thirteen days and nights it journeyed homeward over practically the same route followed by the Presidential train in February, 1861, on its way to the Capital. No pen can ever describe the scenes of sorrow which were witnessed all along the way, not only in Baltimore, Harrisburg, Philadelphia, New York, Albany, Buffalo, Cleveland, Columbus, Indianapolis, and Chicago, where extended stops furnished an opportunity for the people to look upon the face of the stricken leader, but everywhere that the train passed, both by day and night, in country as well as in village and city.

For more than two weeks the friends in Springfield had planned for the sad home-coming. When at nine o'clock on the morning of May 3 the funeral train arrived, the city was crowded with people, many of whom knew Lincoln personally and all of whom honored him while he was living and, now that he was gone, desired to pay sincere tribute to his memory. At home in the State Capitol, where he had witnessed so many stirring scenes in which he, himself, had had a most important part, and where he had so often mingled with the people whom he so dearly loved, his body lay in state. For twenty-four hours, in an unending procession, his friends and neighbors of so many years looked for the last time upon his kindly face.

At ten o'clock on the morning of May 4, the casket was finally closed. Once more a vast procession formed to accompany it—this time to Oak Ridge Cemetery where brief services were held, beautiful in their impressive simplicity. Here Bishop Simpson again spoke in glowing tribute of the dead. Here appropriate hymns were sung and earnest prayers were offered. Here with peculiar fitness the Second Inaugural Address was read. And here the bodies of Abraham Lincoln and his son, William Wallace, familiarly called Willie, whose death more than two years before had so deeply grieved his father's heart, were reverently laid side by side in the receiving tomb.

But the mourning was not by any means confined to these sad rites, nor did it cease with them. The heart of humanity had been deeply touched, and from all sections of the world came messages of loving sympathy to the Government and to the family. One entire volume of more than seven hundred pages of the Diplomatic Correspondence of the year in which Lincoln died, was filled with sympathetic expressions relating to his death. And in all the years that have followed since then, both in the United States and in foreign lands, innumerable monuments have been erected to his memory, the most impressive of all being the Lincoln Memorial at Washington, dedicated May 30, 1922. This beautiful Memorial contains the *Gettysburg Address*, the *Second Inaugural*, and a statue of Abraham Lincoln, over whose head is the inscription:

IN THIS TEMPLE AS IN THE HEARTS OF THE PEOPLE FOR WHOM HE SAVED THE UNION THE MEMORY OF ABRAHAM LINCOLN IS ENSHRINED FOREVER.

Would that this account might end here and that it might be said of Lincoln as was said of another ruler who was foully murdered:

"After life's fitful fever he sleeps well." But this was not to be, for even in the tomb he was not allowed to rest in peace.

On May 11, 1865, the National Lincoln Monument Association was organized for the purpose of erecting a monument to the memory of Abraham Lincoln, late

President of the United States. The first work of this association was the building of a temporary vault, to which the bodies which had been placed in the receiving tomb on May 4, were removed on December 21, 1865. In due course of time the building of the monument was begun and was so far advanced by July 17, 1871, that the remains of Thomas Lincoln, youngest son of the President, who had died in Chicago two days before, were brought to Springfield and placed in one of the crypts. On September 19 of the same year, the remains of President Lincoln and his sons, William and Edward, were also removed to the monument.

On October 9, 1874, the body of President Lincoln was changed from the iron coffin, in which it had rested in the central crypt back of the catacomb, to one of cedar heavily lined with lead. This was placed in a marble sarcophagus which was located in the center of the catacomb, on the north side of the monument. It was from this sarcophagus that an almost successful attempt to steal the body was made on the night of November 7, 1876. The history of this dastardly attempt—one of the most infamous on record, is given in detail in a volume entitled *History of an Attempt to Steal The Body of Abraham Lincoln, Including A History of the Lincoln Guard of Honor with Eight Years' Lincoln Memorial Services*. This volume was printed in 1890 and was edited by John Carroll Power, Custodian of the Lincoln National Monument and Secretary of The Lincoln Guard of Honor. It is chiefly from this History that the information contained in the following summary was secured.

Two motives were back of the plot to steal the body. First, to secure a large reward in money from the government for its return, and second, to obtain a pardon for Benjamin Boyd, a notorious counterfeiter whose arrest in 1875 and sentence to the Joliet penitentiary for ten years had most seriously interfered with the nefarious business of the gang of which he was the leader. The plan was to remove the body to a place near the lake, and there conceal it until the money was paid and the pardon secured.

Terrence Mullen, *alias* T. Durnan, and John Hughes *alias* J. Smith, were the men who conceived this diabolical plot. Lewis C. Swegles, whom they supposed to be in sympathy with them and to whom they revealed the details of their plans, was the one who informed the United States Secret Service of this conspiracy. With his aid the detectives kept in touch with every movement of the conspirators. So it happened that when the latter entered the front coach of the Chicago and Alton train which left Chicago for Springfield the night of November 6, they were not aware of the fact that the former boarded the rear sleeper of the same train. All arrived at Springfield early in the morning of November 7.

Patrick D. Tyrrell, Chief of the Government Secret Service, who had planned and executed the arrest of Benjamin Boyd, the counterfeiter, was also in charge of the plans for the detection and arrest of the conspirators. Swegles remained with them but was in close communication with Chief Tyrrell, who was thus informed regarding all their actions. On the morning of November 7, accompanied by John T. Stuart, Lincoln's first law partner, Tyrrell visited the custodian of the Monument and informed him that two of the conspirators would arrive in the afternoon to inspect the Tomb in preparation for the robbery. The custodian was given an accurate description of them so that they could be easily identified and was directed to answer truthfully all their questions and to extend to them all the courtesies shown to visitors. In due time they arrived, in the persons of Swegles and Hughes, who registered, the first as Henry S. Lewis, Kenosha, Wisconsin and, the second, as James Smith, Racine, Wisconsin.

With all their questions satisfactorily answered, they returned to a hotel in the city to complete their plans. Swegles continued to play the double and dangerous role of a pretended accomplice, who was to furnish a wagon for the removal of the body, while in reality he was a means of communication with the detectives who, late in the evening, went to the Monument, where arrangements had been made with the custodian for their reception.

One of their number was stationed at a point back under the Monument, directly against the wall, on the opposite side of which the sarcophagus was located, in order that he might learn, and at once inform his associates, when the robbers began their work. The other detectives and the custodian were assigned places in Memorial Hall in the south side of the Monument. With Chief Tyrrell standing in a position where he could not be seen but where he could see and hear every movement on the outside, the detectives remained in absolute silence for nearly two hours, when about nine o'clock the thieves appeared on the scene. After carefully inspecting the surroundings, they concluded that all was safe for them to begin the execution of their plans.

In a few minutes, Swegles appeared in front of the door and, giving the password previously agreed upon, reported that Mullen and Hughes had commenced sawing the lock of the door of the catacomb, and at once rejoined them. A little later, the detective who had been stationed against the back wall appeared and announced that work had been begun on the sarcophagus.

For several minutes the detectives anxiously awaited a prearranged signal from Swegles to move upon the robbers and capture them. But he did not appear when expected, for the reason that he had been compelled to stand and hold the dark lantern in an inside corner of the catacomb while Mullen opened the sarcophagus and Hughes patrolled the outside and guarded the door. However, as soon as the sarcophagus was forced open and the coffin partly removed, Swegles was directed to bring up the wagon which he was presumed to have in readiness near by.

Taking advantage of the opportunity thus presented, he went to the door of Memorial Hall on the opposite side of the monument and informed Chief Tyrrell that Mullen and Hughes were waiting at the door of the catacomb for him to bring up the wagon and teamster. Leaving Swegles in the background, the officers started for the catacomb to arrest the robbers and

were surprised not to find them there. Instead of remaining at the door where Swegles had left them, they
had gone a short distance to the north, where they
were waiting for his return. They at first took the
approaching officers to be Swegles and his teamster
coming for the coffin, but soon discovered their mistake. A running fire followed between the robbers
and the officers, in which the former got away and
several of the latter narrowly escaped being killed by
bullets fired both by the robbers and, through mistakes due to the darkness and confusion, by some of
their own number.

The next morning trace of the robbers was found
at a farmhouse, where they had eaten breakfast, about
seven miles from Springfield. They were then lost
sight of for several days. On the evening of November 17, upon information furnished by Swegles, they
were arrested in a saloon kept by Mullen, in Chicago,
and the same night were taken to Springfield.

There was no law at that time under which they
could be sentenced to the penitentiary for the revolting crime which they had attempted. In order
that they might be legally prosecuted, they were
charged with burglary and conspiracy. A special
grand jury was promptly summoned and on November
20, 1876, returned an indictment against Mullen and
Hughes, in which it was charged that on the seventh
day of November, 1876, they "did unlawfully, wick-
edly, knowingly, and feloniously combine, conspire,
and agree together unlawfully and feloniously to steal,
take, and carry away, certain personal goods and

property, to wit: one casket, otherwise called a coffin, of the value of seventy-five dollars, the personal goods and property of the National Lincoln Monument Association, the said Association being then and there organized under the laws of the State of Illinois, contrary to the statutes and against the peace and dignity of the People of the State of Illinois."

After the usual attempts to delay prosecution, including a motion for change of venue to Logan County, once granted and afterward set aside, the trial proceeded, and finally on June 2, 1877, after having been found guilty as charged in the indictment, the defendants, Terrence Mullen *alias* T. Durnan, and John Hughes *alias* J. Smith were sentenced to pay the costs of prosecution and to be confined in the penitentiary of the State of Illinois at Joliet, for the term of one year each, one day of which was to be in solitary confinement, and the balance at hard labor.

After the intense excitement resulting from the attempt to steal the President's body had somewhat subsided, the sarcophagus was repaired and the coffin again placed inside it. Fearing that another attempt to steal it might be made, the coffin was taken out of the sarcophagus and, by the custodian aided by five other trusted friends, was placed in a box and secreted under the monument. There it remained in different places, either resting upon timbers above the ground or buried in the ground, until April 14, 1887, the twenty-second anniversary of the assassination, when it was placed, along with the body of Mrs. Lincoln, in a receptacle under the monument.

On February 12, 1880, The Lincoln Guard of Honor was organized and incorporated under the laws of the State of Illinois. It consisted of nine members, three in addition to the custodian and the five persons referred to in the preceding paragraph. Both the ostensible purpose and the real object of the members of this unique and commendable organization are clearly set forth in the following resolutions unanimously adopted at their ninth and last official annual meeting, held in the Leland Hotel, Springfield, at 8:00 P. M., Monday, February 13, 1888:

WHEREAS, The members of our Society, after the attempt of demons in human form to steal the body of our martyred President, Abraham Lincoln, that they might, by the possession of it, extort gain, having, at the suggestion of an officer of the Lincoln Monument Association, first made the remains temporarily secure, we organized under the laws of the State of Illinois as The Lincoln Guard of Honor, that we might more effectually guard against any further attempts that might be made by vandal hands to rob his tomb; and

WHEREAS, It was obviously indispensable that we should shield the real objects of our origination from the public as the only sure way of accomplishing them, for that reason one of them was made to institute and maintain memorial services on the anniversaries of his birth and death; and

WHEREAS, We have eight times, from 1880 to 1887, inclusive, arranged for and conducted, on the anniversary of his death, each, an increasingly beautiful and impressive memorial service, so that the day has become known as Lincoln Memorial Day; and

WHEREAS, The exhuming of the body of President Lincoln, by The Lincoln Guard of Honor, from the grave where they had secretly buried it years before, and delivering it, April 14, 1887, to the Lincoln Monument Association, before whom it was identified, as attested by a large number of witnesses, and the burial of it with that of his wife, in our presence, in a receptacle prepared under the supervision of our Secretary (as the Custodian of the monument), and encasing them in concrete six by five feet and a half, and eight feet long, with a wall one foot and a half thick of hard burned brick, laid in Portland cement, around that, making the whole equal to a solid mass of stone six feet deep, eight and a half feet wide and eleven feet long, terminates our labors and responsibilities: therefore,

"RESOLVED, That the directors and officers elected at this meeting, being for one year or until their successors are chosen, we will consider their term of office perpetual, if there is not another election; that we will retain our organization under its corporate name as long as there is a member living, and will meet for social or other purposes on the call of any two members, or on the death of a member, as it was, early in our history, mutually agreed that upon the death of any member, the survivors will act as pall-bearers.

"RESOLVED, That we will not again conduct Lincoln Memorial Services, but will leave that to the citizens, or to a new society under another name, and we will heartily join, as citizens, on any Lincoln Memorial Day that they may inaugurate.

"RESOLVED, That our Secretary be, and he is hereby instructed, to have a neat casket made, of sufficient size to contain our record book, certificate of incorporation, seal and press, gavel made of live oak from the steamship of war *Kearsarge*, crimson silk velvet collar covered with patriotic emblems in gold, sent to our Secretary by friends of Lincoln in California, as a mark of their approval of his efforts as Custodian to protect the tomb from desecration, and any papers that it may be desirable to preserve—put all in the casket and keep it in Memorial Hall of the National Lincoln Monument, that they may be left there as mementoes when we cease to use them. On the death of any member, it shall be the duty of any surviving member or members to see that the fact is entered on our record book."

When these resolutions were passed, it was believed that the body of the martyred President had at last found its final resting place. But a little more than a decade later the entire monument had to be taken down and rebuilt with a new foundation on the solid rock. This necessitated the removal of the caskets containing the remains of the Lincoln family to a temporary vault until the reconstructed monument was completed, when they were again replaced in the receptacles prepared for them. This took place September 25, 1901. Mr. J. C. Thompson, legal adviser of the Department of Public Instruction from the State of Illinois, to whom the author is indebted for the information contained in this paragraph, was one of the sixteen friends who were present at the final interment.

To this rebuilt and reconsecrated monument, in ever increasing numbers as the years go by, people from all over the world repair, to pay loving tribute to the memory of Abraham Lincoln, the savior of the Republic—a fulfillment of the prophecy contained in the beautiful Memorial Sermon by Henry Ward Beecher:

"Four years ago, O Illinois, we took from thy midst an untried man, one from among the people; we return him to you a mighty conqueror. Not thine any more, but the nation's; not ours, but the world's. Give him place, O ye prairies! In the midst of this great continent, his dust shall rest, a sacred treasure to myriads who shall pilgrim to that shrine to kindle anew their zeal and patriotism. Ye winds that move over the mighty places of the West, chant his requiem! Ye people, behold the martyr whose blood, as so many articulate words, pleads for fidelity, for law, for liberty!"

INDEX